A Treasure Within

Stories of Remembrance & Rediscovery

Chike Akua

Praise for *A Treasure Within*

"A Treasure Within *is the book that many of us have been waiting for. The deep thinking of Ancient Africa is grasped and communicated clearly through these three powerful stories.*

Families, counselors, teachers, students and the community, in general, can relate directly to these stories. Akua blends his keen perceptions of youth culture and their issues with an authentic African World View, demonstrating its application to the here and now.

It is the writers, artists, dancers, musicians, actors, and playwrights who have always had the power to transmit our deep culture to the masses. It is also our spiritual leaders who have the obligation to be true to our culture.

I am thankful for this outstanding contribution to our mental and spiritual liberation. Our ancestors are pleased. Amun is satisfied."

Asa G. Hilliard III - Nana Baffour Amankwatia II, Ed.D.
Fuller E. Callaway Professor of Urban Education
Georgia State University

"*True to its title,* A Treasure Within *is a gift. Akua weaves adventure, moral lessons, and African history into the everyday lives of his characters. Like Marcus, Imani, and Daniel, the reader emerges from this literary odyssey transformed—never again the same. Parents and teachers,* A Treasure Within *is a must-read for your children.*"

Leslie T. Fenwick, Ph.D,
Professor of Educational Policy, Clark Atlanta University
Visiting Scholar, Harvard Graduate School of Education

"*Chike Akua, a master teacher, engages the reader with three compelling stories. His mastery of the written word intertwined with historical facts and cultural revelations invites the reader to be totally immersed. Readers of all ages will enjoy this literary rites of passage.*"

Phyllis Daniel
Middle School Principal

"Awe-inspiring and filled with enlightenment...young audiences, as well as old will find an eye-opening journey of the spirit within these pages. It is a work that should be read and re-read, for it will have a lasting impact on humanity."

Tavares Stephens, Reading/English Teacher
Author, *The Soulfood Café*

"The magic of these stories is not merely the colorful African characters that come alive, but the principles of a moral life that foster a strong and beautiful spirit. These stories reach beyond the lines of ethnicity and touch the center of the soul."

Marlena Alvarado
English Teacher

"The principles woven into A Treasure Within *provide strength and encouragement in an area of urgent need—the moral development of our children."*

Jackie Miles
Parent

"A Treasure Within *gives young people road maps to follow as they negotiate and navigate through their turbulent and confusing middle years. Akua deals effectively with the inner struggles of his characters. He provides us with stories of youth stumbling under the weight of negative energy, and elders who direct them toward self-awareness, positive self-image, and enlightenment."*

Gwen Russell Green
School Library Media Specialist

Published by
Imani Enterprises
for
Sankofa Educational Services, Inc.
www.imanienterprises.org

Cover illustration
Larry Williams
Layout and design
BestPrint & Design

ISBN 0-9704644-1-x

Funding for *A Treasure Within* was provided in part
by the following African American businesses:
The MATAH Network
C.D. Moody Construction Company
KACO Supply Company

Special thanks to the following families
for their generous support:
Jason & Nitza Fenwick
Wayne & Bianca Hamilton
Michael & Tamura Lomax

For Jahbari

"Go back, Black
(Africa, Africa)
Go Back, Black
Know Yourself,
Touch Yourself,
See Yourself,
Be Yourself."

—Amiri Baraka

Other Books by Chike Akua

A Treasure Within:
Parent/Teacher Resource Guide (2001)

A Kwanzaa Awakening:
Lessons for the Children (2000)

A Million Under One:
One Man's Perspective on the Million Man March
(1996)

The Autobiography of the
African American Self
(Justin Fenwick, TPFS Press, 1995)

See Order form on last page

CONTENTS

In Memory of

Kris Henderson
&
Jory Thomas

To the Reader

It is not by chance

that this book has come into your possession.

You are about to embark upon a journey

that will re-introduce you to the

true essence of

who you are.

Read and be wise.

sankofa

"...to return to the past
is the
first step forward."

I

Marcus Strong's eyes were wide with excitement, as the final bell was about to ring. Finally, the end of seventh period. He didn't have much homework and was looking forward to finishing it quickly so he could meet the rest of the guys out on the neighborhood basketball court. They had a score to settle. Who was the best player? Who had the best ball handling skills? Who had the best jumper? Who had the best leaping ability? To sum it all up, who had that unique ability to take the game to the next level and score at will? All the brothers had been talking trash all day. But Marcus knew he was among the best, if not *the* best.

This wasn't all he looked forward to. After all, it was the end of May—countdown to the end of the school year. Marcus daydreamed through the last two periods of the day thinking how wonderful summer was going to be. If his grades were right, Mom and Dad had promised to pay for him to go to a one-week basketball camp. And Marcus had seen to it that the grades *were* right. All A's and B's, except for a C in English. But if he turned in his extra credit report to Mr. Freeman, that *C* was guaranteed to magically transform into a *B*.

"What's so bad about a *C*?" he remembered asking his Dad after he brought home the last progress report. "Is it your best?" His father replied.

"Well, no, but—"

"No *but's*, a *C* is average, it's in the middle, just as close to the bottom as it is to the top. It's unacceptable Marcus. In fact, you *should* be making an *A*. You ought to feel fortunate that Mr. Freeman gave you the opportunity to do an extra credit report to bring it up. Make sure you do it. Make sure it's your best. And make sure you turn it in on time!"

Dad didn't play when it came to grades. Neither did Mom. But in Marcus' mind, it was all good. "All I have to do is finish typing the summary and the title page and I'm finished," he thought to himself. Marcus had zoned out for quite some time. He was zoning back in just in time to hear Mrs. Ashanti say, "You all know that there have been several suspensions in the past few days. Too many brothers and sisters are not showing self-control, getting into fights over foolishness. Control your flow of energy. If you discipline yourself, others won't have to. I don't want to hear about any of you getting in trouble."

This was the standard line Mrs. Ashanti used. She had taught them all about energy in Science class, how it was conducted and how the human body was basically a conductor of energy. One must control their flow of energy. Just then, the bell rang and everyone carefully proceeded to the door in measured strides. No one dared run because Mrs. Ashanti would make that person sit down until everyone else had gone.

Once outside the door, Marcus made a beeline straight for his locker. He was on a mission. "Get your things and get home before four. Finish your homework so you can meet the guys at five," he thought.

Just as that thought was completing itself in his mind—

WHAM!!!

Marcus went flying off his feet. His books, notebooks, pens and pencils flew everywhere. He looked up to see James looking down at him. James had been running through the hall at breakneck speed and ran into him.

"Yo man! Why don't you watch where you're goin'!" snapped Marcus, picking himself up.

"Man, shut up!" said James sucking his teeth.

Marcus shot back a glare that said that

he meant business. James got the eye message and replied, "What's up then?! You wanna do something?!"

By this time a crowd was gathering. Marcus was up and the two boys stood toe-to-toe in each others' faces.

"I know you ain't gonna take that, Marcus," instigated one of the boys in the crowd. Marcus' eyes narrowed and tunnel vision began to set in. All he could see was the spot on James' eye he intended to swell with his fist.

"What's up?!" said James as he pushed Marcus backwards. Just as Marcus lunged forward to attack, Mr. Freeman grabbed him from behind.

"Alright! Break it up!" said Mr. Freeman.

"You're lucky he held you back," yelled James.

Marcus eyes turned to fire. He broke from Mr. Freeman's grip just long enough to catch the corner of James jaw with a left hook.

Mr. Freeman grabbed him and held him, this time more firmly. James was holding his jaw. By this time another teacher had arrived and was holding James, too. Mr. Freeman escorted Marcus to the office.

"I'm gonna miss my bus," cried Marcus.

"That's the last thing you need to worry about right now. I'm sure your parents will be picking you up today," said Mr. Freeman.

"But it was his fault! He started it! I was just going to my locker!"

"You had a chance to let it go, but you just *had* to take that last swing, didn't you?!"

Marcus sat in the office enraged. A storm of emotions clouded his face and his stomach was turning with fury. It all happened so quickly. Just a moment ago he was daydreaming about finishing his paper and playing basketball. Now he was in the office. Once his parents found out about what happened, he might not be able to do anything for the rest of the school year *and* the summer.

II

Marcus' father, Mr. Strong, had a serious presence. The same fire that filled Marcus' eyes a moment before could now be seen in his father's eyes as he entered the main office.

"My name is Mr. Strong, I'm here to see my son Marcus," he told the secretary.

"Right this way," she replied.

Marcus hung his head in shame. How would he explain? It wasn't his fault. Or was it? He couldn't even look at his father in the eye when he came in the room. He put his face in his hands.

"How are you doing, Mr. Strong?" said Mr. Freeman.

"Fine," said Mr. Strong.

"I'm sorry I had to meet with you under these circumstances, but Marcus had a little problem today."

"What happened?" asked Mr. Strong.

"Marcus got into a fight with another young man," replied Mr. Freeman.

"But he pushed me over and got in my face and—

"Hoold up!" said Mr. Freeman. "Slow

down and take it from the top."

"What happened?" asked Mr. Strong again, this time a bit more sternly.

Marcus took a deep breath, trying to regain his composure.

"I was going to my locker just after the bell rang," Marcus began slowly. "Just as I was getting to my locker, James ran right into me and knocked me down. Then he got in my face like he wanted to fight me. It wasn't my fault."

"Mr. Strong, we got there in time to break it up, but Marcus took a swing anyway. He hit the other boy in the face," said Mr. Freeman.

Mr. Strong looked at Marcus.

"Yeah but—

Mr. Strong simply held up his hand as if to say, "don't say another word."

Marcus hung his head again. He wanted to cry. How did such a promising afternoon turn out to be so terrible?

"I'm afraid that's going to be three days out-of-school suspension," said Mr. Freeman. "James will be dealt with, too." Marcus knew he was not only going to suffer the school's punishment, but he also had to face the wrath of his father.

III

"Come down to the kitchen, Marcus," yelled Mr. Strong up the stairs. Marcus came down the steps slowly to see his father sitting at the dinner table. The table was spread with a tossed salad, wheat rolls, and a pitcher of iced tea. His mother was placing a dish of beans and rice on the table and taking her seat.

"What happened, Dear?" said Mrs. Strong.

"Ma, I swear, I didn't—

"No need to swear, Sweetheart. Just tell me what happened."

Marcus ran down the whole story. His mother listened intently.

"He asked for it!" Marcus concluded.

Mr. Strong stopped in mid-air with a fork full of beans and rice.

"What did you say?"

"I mean—

"What could you have done to avoid this whole thing, Marcus?" asked Mr. Strong in a stern voice. "I know the boy ran into you. I understand he even had an attitude about it. Sounds like that boy didn't have any sense. But did you have to act like you didn't have any sense either?! Was there any way you could have responded differently?"

"Dad, you don't understand..." pleaded Marcus.

"No son, apparently *you* don't understand. Mr. Strong was visibly upset, yet he carefully controlled his voice to keep from yelling. "You did not weigh your options before acting. You didn't think about the consequences."

"Your father is right, Marcus," said Mrs. Strong. "You had a chance to walk away, but your pride got in the way."

Marcus fell silent. It was going to be a long three days at home on suspension.

"Tomorrow, I'm going up to school to get your work for the next three days from your teachers," said Mr. Strong. "Then I will give you *my* list of work. And you know the rest: no TV, no video games, no telephone, and *definitely*, no basketball."

Marcus sat on the side of his bed as Mr. Strong entered the room.

"Son, turn your Bible to the Book of Proverbs, chapter 25, verse 28."

Marcus picked up his book of Scriptures

and turned to the appointed verse and read, *"He that hath no rule over his own spirit is like a city that is broken down, and without walls."*

"This afternoon, you suffered an attack from the enemy," began Mr. Strong. *"You* were the city with no walls, son. James was not the enemy. He's just another lost brother seeking a false sense of manhood *just as you were.* Your anger was the enemy and you allowed it to take control of your spirit."

"Dad, how can I control my anger and still get the respect I deserve? I'm not the type to go around starting fights. You know I'm not like that. But I wanted him to know he couldn't just knock me over and keep on going."

"Soon Son, you will learn how to carry yourself in such a way that demands the respect you're seeking. Soon you will learn how to fight with your mind."

Marcus looked disappointed. He was expecting a more direct answer. His father sensed his disappointment.

"Let's pray. You've got a lot of work to do in the morning."

They both knelt down at the side of the bed.

"Dear Lord," began Mr. Strong. "We thank you for all of your blessings. We thank you for a roof over our heads and food on our table. We thank you for providing our every need. We thank you for giving us guidance through the good times and the bad. We thank you for the example that Our Ancestors gave us. We thank you for giving us life to continue their struggle. We thank you for the triumphs and victories as well as the trials and tribulations. For it is in difficult times that we learn the greatest and most enduring lessons. So we even thank you for what happened this afternoon. For there is a lesson to be learned. What appears to be intended for evil, we know you intended it for good.

"Lord, bless our family and give Marcus guidance. Keep your hand upon him and your hedge of protection around him. Help him see the mighty work that you're going to do through him to help our people and humanity, Lord. It is time, Lord. *It is time.* In your Holy and Righteous Name we pray. Amen."

They got off their knees and Marcus climbed into bed. As Mr. Strong was about to turn off the light, Marcus said, "Thanks for the prayer, Dad."

"You're welcome."

"Dad...what did you mean when you said, 'it's time'."

Mr. Strong had an expression on his face that seemed to speak with the timeless wisdom

of the ages. He turned off the lights. "You'll
see, son. You'll see."

IV

Marcus began to drift off to sleep. As his consciousness ebbed away, he felt himself rising slowly. He wasn't quite asleep. He was in that awkward timeless moment between the sleeping state and the waking state. He was rising, slowly being separated from his body. He was being transported to another place and another time. He was traveling. He was being drawn like a magnet.

His spirit felt lighter than the air as he passed into another dimension. At first it seemed devoid of time and space. But then images began to solidify and take shape. He looked down and saw sand. He looked up and saw a few clouds hovering above. He looked off in the distance and saw the sun slowly rising in the midst of three pyramids.

The sky was all golden with burnt orange highlights cascading through the lining of the few clouds. The polished limestone of the pyramids was gleaming white and sparkling in the sun. Around the pyramids was a great city.

It all seemed to be so distant but so close. So near and yet so far. The mystical appearance of this place was striking.

Some time passed as Marcus continued looking in the sky marveling at his surroundings. The arid sands beneath his feet became hotter and hotter. As he looked off in the distance, all he could see was sand and more sand. Sand hills and sand dunes. The sunlight reflecting off the sand was brilliant and blinding. Marcus began to walk. He didn't know where to walk or what direction to go in, but he just walked. Should he go toward the pyramids or off in another direction. He knew he couldn't just stand still, motion was a must.

The sun seemed to get hotter and hotter. He began to sweat profusely. He reached down to wipe his face. He felt a tattered piece of cloth where his shirt should have been. He looked down to find himself clothed in dirty rags. His mouth was dry and tasted like sand. How he longed for water to cool his face and tongue.

Then, off in the distance, a few rays of sunlight came together to create an image. The image began to move slowly yet very intently toward Marcus. He wanted to turn and take cover, but all of a sudden, he could not seem to move. He was under the power of this image that was approaching. Finally, the image materialized.

It took the form of a man. An elder. He was tall and thin with a gray beard and a round halo-like white afro. The contrast of his dark skin and his white hair made quite a sight. He was clothed in a long ornate white garment trimmed in gold. In his right hand was a staff with an ankh on the top, held securely in his hand. Marcus had seen this symbol before. He remembered that it was a symbol which represented life. The man did not seem to be the least bit fazed by the heat. He seemed to be comfortable and at peace.

Marcus wanted to speak, but his mouth was so dry, he *couldn't* speak. Even trying to swallow made him give a weak, dry cough. The man pulled out a drinking gourd from a pouch which he carried on one shoulder. He held it in his left hand. Then he began to wave his right hand over the top of the drinking gourd. It looked almost as though he was sprinkling something inside of it, yet nothing was coming out of his hand. He then handed the gourd to Marcus and said, "Drink."

The man's voice was deep and rich.

Weak and bent over, Marcus took the gourd and drank. As he drank the sweet waters, he felt himself being restored to strength. The man took out a cloth and took the gourd. He poured some of the water on the cloth. Then he wiped Marcus' face. Marcus felt like a new person—refreshed and rejuvenated. Now the sun didn't seem to be so hot anymore. He could once again appreciate the beauty of the sky now that he was no longer in distress.

"Hotep," greeted the man.

"Huh?!" replied a bewildered Marcus.

"Hotep means 'peace'. Peace be unto you."

"Oh...peace to you, Sir...and thank you for your help," replied Marcus with all due respect. He knew how to treat his elders. "Where am I?"

"You are in the ancient land of your Foremothers and Forefathers. It is the Motherland. We call this part of the land Kemet."

"Who are you?" asked Marcus.

"I was just going to ask you the same question, my son." smiled the elder.

"My name is Marcus."

"I already know your name, young brother. I even know who you are. I am simply asking you to see if *you* know who you are."

Marcus didn't say a word. He just looked confused.

"My name is Ptahotep. I was sent to guide you on this journey. I am a scribe in the king's court. I copy the Holy Writings called the *medu neter* for the king. I teach the youth who they are. I train them up in the way that they should go that they should never depart from it."

"Why am I here...I thought I was asleep," asked Marcus.

"*You* are not asleep, *your body* is. *You* are very awake right now. You have been brought back here to learn certain lessons to complete your mission. *It is time.* I am here to help you remember that which is buried deep within. It is your hidden treasure. You have been clothed within and without in the raiment of your Ancestors."

Marcus looked down and saw himself wrapped in a long, white and gold knee-length dashiki and wide leg drummer pants. A pair of comfortable sandals were strapped around his feet which had nearly been burned by the sand. A matching kufi sat perched on top of his head. He looked at himself in awe.

"Come...for this sacred time is of the essence, and there is none to waste," said Ptahotep.

They entered the ornate gates of the city. There were statues and stone structures all over. They passed many other people who were dressed like Ptahotep. They passed through a marketplace area. There were fruits and vegetables for sale. There were pieces of bright, colorful looking cloth displayed, as well. They came upon a large temple-looking structure. It was gigantic. It was easy to see that this colossal structure was designed with the most advanced architectural knowledge and that the materials used were the finest in the land. On each side of the doorway, there was a square, slim stone pole that came to a point at the top. It had strange writings on each side. It looked like a small Washington Monument. Marcus remembered that Mr. Freeman had told him that the Washington Monument was a design taken from ancient African obelisks. As they walked through the doorway, Marcus looked up and noticed more of the strange writings just above the doorway. He couldn't read it at first and suddenly his mind began to transform. He was now able to somehow read this language that he had never seen before. The inscription above the doorway read, "Know thyself." He said nothing, but kept on walking with Ptahotep, his Ancestral Guide.

"This is the Temple of Ipet Isut in the grand city of Waset," said Ptahotep. It is one of the first universities built by your Ancestors. It is where over 80,000 people from Our Motherland and from around the world have come to study the Sacred Sciences. Others have called what we study here 'the mystery system' because the higher knowledge that I am about to share with you remains a mystery to so many."

Marcus was speechless.

They entered a large sanctuary with a domed ceiling. Marcus saw dozens of children sitting on the floor with their legs crossed. Each had in their lap a clay tablet. Each child was writing on the clay tablet and taking instruction from a master teacher.

Ptahotep turned to Marcus and handed him a tattered scroll of papyrus.

"Open," said Ptahotep.

As Marcus opened the scroll, he saw magnificent writings but he couldn't comprehend it.

"What does it say?" he asked.

"Read it," said Ptahotep.

"But I don't know this language," replied Marcus.

"Nonsense. You just read the inscription above the doorway."

Marcus looked at his Ancestral Guide with amazement.

"All you have to do is look at it and allow your Ancestral memory to reveal what it says."

Marcus looked again. Just as before, something began to transform in his mind. Somehow, he began to understand what it said. He read the first line on the scroll.

"It says, 'when the student is ready, a

teacher shall appear'."

"Yes," said Ptahotep. *You* are ready and *I* have appeared. *It is time.* What you are about to learn shall give you guidance for the rest of your life and even beyond. As long as you guard this knowledge, it will be a lamp unto your feet providing light in the midst of darkness."

"What is the first principle that is written?"

"The wise one," Marcus struggled to interpret the writings, "has control of thought."

"There are many forces competing for control of your mind, young brother. Sound thinking produces sound words. Sound words produce sound actions. As you can see, it is a process and a cycle. But if the thinking is out of order then everything else will be out of order."

"I see a lot of my friends who are not in control of their minds. They act certain ways just to get the attention of others. They're trying to be something they're not. Like the boy James I got into a fight with—he tries to act like a thug or something. But he's not really like that. He just tries to act that way to impress people."

"Only a fool is impressed with ignorance. But what about you, young brother? You lost control, too. If only you and James had been in the hallway alone without others instigating and egging you on to fight, would you have fought?"

"Probably not," replied Marcus. "I mean...you know...you want everybody to see you beat somebody up so you get more respect. If nobody sees it..."

"Only people who have something to prove are willing to fight over foolishness. You had something to prove to *yourself.* If you were truly confident, you would not have felt the need to fight and prove your ability to fight. And, Brother Marcus, there are many other ways to get respect."

"I don't understand," said Marcus.

"Perhaps you will when you read the second principle."

"The wise one has control of their actions."

"Come," said Ptahotep. "We must travel to the city of Beni Hasan."

With that, Ptahotep flung his hand in Marcus' face as if he were washing a window. Marcus' reflex and response was to lean back and blink. After he blinked, he was in a new place.

"What happened? Where are we?"

"You are in the ancient city of Beni Hasan. It is in another part of Kemet. We must go into the temple."

As they entered the temple, Marcus saw more of the sacred writings on the walls.

"What does this place have to do with the second principle?"

"Look at the writings on the wall. What do they look like?"

"They look like people fighting and wrestling. Hey...! See there! African people used to fight, too!"

"A fool looks with ignorance and sees a lie. It is a wise one who can look with insight and see Truth. What you are looking at is not the immature and irrational violence that you often see in your day and age. What you are looking at are the origins of martial arts."

"What do you mean? I thought Chinese and Japanese people came up with that stuff."

"No, my son. Our Asian brothers and sisters certainly learned it well. They took it and mastered it as we did. The martial arts were not about going around and showing off that you could beat people up. That is the sport of fools and most of what you have seen in movies does not capture the essence of the art. The martial arts were for the purpose of controlling and mastering the life-force energy within you. The goal was *not* to fight. The goal was actually *never* to fight. If you fought, it showed that you lacked the discipline to control a situation without fighting."

"Why would somebody practice all those

deadly skills and then not use them?"

"The greatest and most difficult battle a person can ever fight is against the enemy within."

"So a warrior had to control his actions?" Marcus though out loud.

"A warrior had to control his actions and only use his physical skills when defending his family or his people. Is that what you were engaged in when you fought James?" asked Ptahotep.

Marcus couldn't reply. He only hung his head.

"Just as your mother told you, you were only fighting in defense of your false pride."

"So what should I have done?"

"If you meet a person who challenges you and displays his ignorance, pay no attention to his evil speech. If you do not confront him while he is raging, people will call him an ignoramus. Your self-control will be a match for his evil utterances."

"But it's not easy to sit there and let somebody talk about you and challenge you without doing anything...especially when you know you can beat the person."

"Young brother, the principles I am teaching you are as old as the hills. They shall continue to endure beyond your lifetime. They are not easy, but they are enduring. Wickedness and foolishness are but for a short time, but righteousness shall endure forever. You must walk with a peace that surpasses all understanding...and a peace which surpasses all *misunderstandings*."

"You said *hotep* means peace, right?" asked Marcus.

"Yes."

"Does that have anything to do with your name...Ptahotep?"

"Yes. *Ptah* is one of the names of the Creator and *hotep* means peace. My name means, *the peace of God*. This is why I am here...to teach you the lesson of what it means to walk in peace."

"But I'm living in such a violent world. I mean...every minute you hear of somebody dying and getting killed. Fights get started so quickly, just like mine."

"This is precisely the reason why *you* must walk in peace. The supreme art of war is to subdue the enemy without fighting. One day you might even win your enemy as a friend."

V

*O*ff in the distance, Marcus saw another huge temple, but this one was carved into the side of a mountain. Then suddenly, this temple came rushing toward him. What was miles away was now right in front of him. He jumped back in amazement. There were people walking in and out of the temple.

"There may be some things that are unclear to you. Perhaps one of my friends can teach you this particular lesson better than I can," said Ptahotep.

As Ptahotep said this, a woman emerged from the temple. She wore the headdress of a queen. Her long, white gown was embroidered with red, gold, black, and purple. It shimmered in the light. She was so beautiful and so elegant. Her skin was velvety Black. The gold around her neck and on her wrists gleamed in the noonday sun. She had some sort of aura around her. She was truly magnificent. Marcus dropped the scroll Ptahotep had given him, then clumsily picked it up.

"Hotep, Queen Sister," said Ptahotep as he bowed.

"Peace be unto you, Brother Ptahotep," she said bowing in return. Her voice was like many waters, rich and deep.

"I have here a seeker of knowledge named Marcus who has come to learn the meaning of peace."

"Ahh, you have come to the right place, Marcus. I am Queen Hatshepsut."

"Pleased to meet you your majesty," said Marcus. He bowed as best he could. He had never met a queen before or bowed to anyone before, but he was so impressed that he didn't want to offend her.

"Queen Hatshepsut was Pharaoh of all the land at one time," said Ptahotep.

"But I thought only men could be Pharaohs," said Marcus.

"Marcus, as a Woman, I am Queen of the Earth and the Mother of Humanity. Do you think I am not fit to govern the greatest kingdom the world has ever known?"

"No," said Marcus apologetically. "I mean...I didn't mean it like that. Yeah...you could rule...but..."

"I know you have learned little about the majesty and wisdom of Women. So many of my sisters carry themselves as much less than the Queens and Princesses they are. But I ruled for over 20 years. Do you know what people remember most about my reign?"

"What?"

"Peace. While I sat on the throne there was not one war in all the land. We made our enemies respect us without hurting or killing them. I could have given orders to my soldiers to destroy many of the surrounding nations, but peace was the order of the day. It is our duty to restore peace to the world which is in need of great healing. Things are out of order, Brother Marcus. We must make peace the order of the day once again."

"Thank you for your words of wisdom, Queen Sister," said Ptahotep.

"I must go now, brothers. Many of my sisters need the wisdom I am sharing with you. Peace be with you." She walked off into the air as elegantly as she had appeared.

"Peace be with you, too," said Marcus.

"Don't be so taken with the Queen's beauty that you miss the wisdom of her words, young brother. You must treat all of your sisters with the respect you gave her *even* if they don't show themselves that kind of respect. What is the next principle?"

Marcus looked down at the scroll again.

"*The wise one has devotion of purpose*. What purpose are they talking about?"

"You tell me," replied Ptahotep. What is

your purpose in life as an individual and what is the collective purpose of African people?"

"I don't know," said Marcus. "How am I supposed to know that?"

"Ah, but you *do* know. What did your father tell you?"

"He said that he and my mom named me *Marcus* after Marcus Garvey, the great Black leader who tried to unite Africans worldwide. He said my purpose in life was to carry on Garvey's work of restoring African people to their traditional greatness."

"So then you *do* know your purpose. This principle says that you must be devoted to your purpose and never stray from it. You were sent to earth at a particular time and to a particular place for a very special reason. Everyone has a very special purpose. Many people are so blind that they can never see what is right in front of them."

"But there are so many people who don't even want to do right. They won't listen to me."

"There are infinitely more who are looking for your rise and will follow you if you commit yourself to righteousness. All you have to do is lead by example. But you must have devotion of purpose. And Brother, Marcus, not only must we restore *our* people to their traditional greatness. We must restore humanity. In order to do this, you must have devotion of purpose."

"But I'm just one person. One person can't make that much of a difference," said Marcus.

"Tell that to Martin Luther King. Tell that to Nelson Mandela. Tell that to Harriet Tubman. Tell it to Sojourner Truth. Or shall we go back to visit Queen Hatshepsut so you can tell her that?" challenged Ptahotep. "Yes, Brother. You are only one person...you are one person who understands very little about the power within you to affect the world. The Creator placed this power deep within you."

"I feel most powerful when I'm on the basketball court and the ball is in my hands. I feel like I can do anything with the ball. I can create shots. I can drive to the basket. I can pass the ball; whatever it takes to win. It doesn't even matter whose guarding me. I'm in control."

"Ohh, Brother Marcus," said Ptahotep closing his eyes. It was as if he was visualizing something. "This feeling of complete power and control that you feel on the court is the same power and authority that you must exercise off the court. My son, the ball is in your hands and time is running out." Ptahotep looked deeply into Marcus' eyes. The looked penetrated all his weaknesses and fears until it lay hold of the power within.

"Do you see what I see?" said Ptahotep.

"I feel like I'm discovering a part of myself that I didn't even know existed," said Marcus.

"This is why you have been brought here."

VI

Marcus looked down at the scroll to see what the next principle was. When he looked back up, he and Ptahotep were back at the first temple they had visited. He was beginning to get used to the time travel, but a little shaken at how sudden it always occurred.

"Could you let me know when you're going to whisk me away to another place. It's weird when things change so quickly."

"Things are going to change much more quickly in the world you live in if our people are not awakened, young brother. But the change will be for the worse."

"Can't you just talk like regular people?"

"I'm not like regular people...and neither are you, my son. What's the fourth principle?"

"The next principle says, *the wise one has faith in the ability of the teacher to teach the Truth.* Now we need to talk about this one. I mean... I've had some teachers I trust, but I've also had some teachers that I don't trust at all. A lot of teachers I've had don't even care about me. It seems like they're just there to get a paycheck."

"That may be so, brother. But what about

the ones who *do* care. What about Mr. Freeman and Mrs. Ashanti and the others. A teacher can only teach you what you *allow* them to teach you. You must allow them to draw out the very best that is within you. And when you have a teacher that you don't particularly care for, that doesn't mean that you can't learn some valuable lessons from them. Also, that doesn't mean you can disrespect them just because you may not like them. You must never disrespect your teachers. Remember what you read to me earlier: *when the student is ready, a Teacher shall appear.* You have the ability to draw to yourself the type of teachers you will need to complete your mission. It is about knowing how to use the power within."

Marcus looked perplexed.

"All these powers you keep saying that I have...what's that all about? This isn't a cartoon... I'm not a superhero. I'm only human."

"Your response is not incorrect, but it is *incomplete*. Yes, you're human, but you are also Divine. You were created in the image of the Most High. You have deep within you the powers of the Most High. For those powers to come forth, you must commit yourself to righteousness especially when it's most difficult."

"Why is everything all about the Most High and the Creator here? I mean...don't get me wrong, I believe in God and I even go to church, but..."

"Young warrior, you can never separate the legacy of your Ancestors from their abiding faith in the Creator. In the time and place that you are now living, the people of all nations have forgotten their Source. This is why there is so much calamity, death, and destruction. You must not make the same mistake. It is not the way of your people. Your people have always given praises to the Most High. Your people have always served the Most High. You must follow in the footsteps of your people. And remember, to believe is not enough. You must follow the righteous path."

"So what are the fifth and sixth principles talking about: *The wise one must have faith in himself to learn the Truth and faith in herself to live the Truth.* What exactly is Truth?"

"Look up," replied Ptahotep.

Marcus looked up.

"Now look down."

Marcus looked down. In that short period of time he was taken up on a cliff. He looked across the canyon in front of him and about a mile away he could see the other side of the cliff.

It made him nervous since he was slightly

afraid of heights.

"No need to be afraid. We'll only be here a moment. You see Marcus, there is a vast chasm or gap between what we know and what we *do*. We can know something is right, but we might not necessarily *do it*. That's what this canyon represents: it is the gap between what we *should* do and what we *actually* do."

"How do I bridge the gap," asked Marcus intently. "I wanna do the right thing, but sometimes it's tough."

"What bridges the gap is submission."

"What does that mean?"

"You must allow your Higher Self to control your lower self. Your lower self will get you into all sorts of trouble if you let it. But your Higher Self is that part of you that wants to do right. Don't let your lower self control you. Let your Higher Self have its way."

"People are gonna think I'm some sort of punk if I do all this stuff you're telling me."

"Brother Marcus, your lower self is speaking."

"But I don't want people calling me lame. And I definitely don't want people treating me that way."

"This is why principles *seven* and *eight* are so important," said Ptahotep.

"*The wise one has freedom from resentment*

under the experience of persecution and freedom from resentment under the experience of wrong," read Marcus.

"Yes. If you will have the courage to be who you truly are, it will give others the courage to stop wearing the mask and do the same. There will be those who try to test you, but with your wisdom you will rise above their ignorance and serve as an example for them to better themselves. In the end you will be highly respected."

"All these things that you're teaching me are heavy. I feel like my mind is about to overflow. I mean...I appreciate it and everything, but I hope I can live up to your expectations."

"It is not my expectations you should be living up to, young warrior. It is the expectations of the Creator who created you and me both. Principles nine and ten deal with the ability to distinguish between right and wrong and the willingness to operate with a sense of values. You know the difference between right and wrong. Your struggle will be your willingness to operate with the values that you have been taught."

"You're right. Sometimes its tough when you stand alone in the middle of a bunch of people who want to do wrong."

"My son, know that you are never alone.

Your Ancestors watch over you. The Most High watches over you and has dispatched others to give you guidance. You are *never* alone."

"I want to do the things my parents have taught me. But it seems like there are a lot of people who haven't been taught the values that I have."

"The values that our people have taken on since we were stolen from the Motherland are not the original values we had. This is why you were brought here. We must all return at one time or another. We must return to the source. Remember, submission is the key. Look over there and see what happens when we submit to our Higher Self."

Ptahotep pointed in the direction of the other side of the canyon. Slowly the other side began to move toward them, bridging the gap of the deep canyon between.

"It is through submission to the Higher Self that we bridge the gap between what we *should* do and what we *actually* do," said Ptahotep. "Come we must return to the temple."

They walked from the two cliffs which had been joined together. Marcus' mind was still putting together the miracle which Ptahotep had performed in front of him.

They entered the large doors of the temple. As he took in Ptahotep's words, he looked around the temple at the young students sitting on the floor writing on their clay tablets. They were so attentive to the teacher's instructions. "So what about James," he said. "Will anyone teach him the things that you have taught me?"

"Look. Ptahotep pointed to the children sitting on the floor. Just then one of them turned around and looked at Marcus. It was James. He had a surprised and sorry look on his face—just like Marcus.

"There are yet many more we must bring here in the millennium and beyond to remind them of who they are. You and James are but two among many."

"When I found you, young Marcus, you were thirsty and I gave you water to drink. You were dirty and I helped to clean your face. You did not know in which direction to go and I gave you guidance. This now, is the task before you—to do unto others as I have done unto you. The life you are living is like walking through a dry, arid desert. You must provide people with the living water of knowledge and enlightenment; for the people are destroyed for lack of knowledge. You must give them guidance and point them in the direction of others who can give right guidance. You must help people to clean themselves up in a world in which people's lifestyles have become filthy."

As Marcus thought about the depth of Ptahotep's words, immediately it was pitch dark.

"Hey...what happened!" Marcus couldn't even see his hand in front of his face. Then, he saw the faintest light and a very dim silhouette of Ptahotep. Ptahotep's hands were outstretched in front of him. The dim light was coming from his hands which were held shut together. He slowly opened and cupped his hands. In his hand a small flame emerged. It began to cast a brilliant light. He held it out to Marcus. As Marcus reached for it slowly in awe, Ptahotep explained, "This flame represents your spirit. It is your life-force energy. You can see how this small flame gave light in the midst of a total and complete darkness. This is the power you have within. But be mindful, young warrior. Fire can be used to bring warmth and to bring light...or it can be used to burn, kill, and destroy. How will you use your fire inside, young warrior?"

With that, he flung the tiny flame into the sky and it burst into a magnificent light called the sun.

"You are the light of the world, young brother. Let your light shine," called Ptahotep as he turned and walked away. "Shemhotep."

"Huh?...wait a minute...what does that

mean?" pleaded Marcus.

"Walk in peace."

VII

"ime to get up Marcus," said Mr. Strong. Marcus opened his eyes. He looked tired and confused. "Are you alright, you look like you had a visitation in your sleep." Mr. Strong smiled.

Marcus didn't say anything, he just looked at the grin on his father's face and wondered if his father knew anything about what he'd just experienced. Was it a dream? It seemed so real.

When Marcus returned to school after his suspension, there was a great deal of talk about the showdown between him and James. Marcus ignored the taunts and instigation. He went to Mr. Freeman's room just before first period.

"Marcus! Good to have you back, brother," said Mr. Freeman.

"Hey, Mr. Freeman," he replied. "Here's my extra credit report." Just then he caught a glimpse of a book on the corner of Mr. Freeman's desk. It said: *The Teachings of Ptahotep: The Oldest Book in the World.*

"Where did you get this book from, Mr. Freeman?"

"From the Black to Basics Bookstore. You know...over on Independence Ave. It's a good book, Brother. It is the oldest *complete* text in the world. It was written over 4300 years ago in ancient Kemet. You might want to check it out sometime. Lots of wisdom in it."

Marcus smiled inwardly. He had already checked it out...and learned a great deal from it.

"I'll see you later, Mr. Freeman."

Marcus left Mr. Freeman's room and, as he neared his locker, there was a small crowd gathering as if they were expecting something to happen. When they moved out of the way, Marcus saw James at his locker.

They looked each other squarely in the eye.

Marcus said, "What's up, Brother?"

"Hotep, Brother?" said James. And they shook hands and embraced.

A Reason for Being

I

Imani Johnson sat still thinking deeply about what was being said. It was a warm Thursday evening in the fellowship hall of her church. Every Thursday the Sankofa Youth Group would have its weekly rap session. This week, the topic was dating. The discussion had been lively. Though usually somewhat outspoken, Imani listened quietly and intently. The group of 13 boys and girls ranged in age from 12 - 18. Imani had been one of the girls who asked Pastor Reed to come up with a forum for the kids of the church to discuss issues involving growing up and being a conscious productive citizen. Pastor Reed liked the idea and soon the church gave birth to the Sankofa Youth Group.

With some research and help from Pastor Reed, they had decided on this name because of its deep meaning. Sankofa was a symbol and word used among the Akan people in Ghana, West Africa. It meant "to go back to the past is the first step forward." They agreed with Pastor Reed that they, as youth, needed to know about their past in order to chart a successful future. Imani was proud about how the group had grown from two girls and one boy to 13 committed young people who often brought friends to the meetings.

This week's discussion about male/female relationships and dating was hitting on some issues that were very close to home. Bro. Kwame, the youth minister led the discussion. He was in his early twenties and had just recently graduated from college. He was working as a teacher at the local elementary school. He was clean-cut, tall and lean with a thin mustache and a short round afro. Bro. Kwame talked about the things young people should be aware of when dating. He warned the brothers to be careful of young sisters who were flirtatious.

One young brother, Antonio, raised his hand and said that some sisters were always saying suggestive things to him and his friends. "Sometimes girls write nasty notes and stuff. What should I do if this sister is just throwing herself at me?"

"If somebody threw you a raw piece of meat would you eat it?" replied Bro. Kwame.

"No!" said the boy.

"Why not?"

"Cuz. It's not done, it needs to be cooked. I could get sick if I ate a raw piece of meat," replied the boy.

"The same is true when you engage in premarital sex. It can do damage to your spirit just the way a raw piece of meat can damage your body. A woman and a man were not meant to be involved that way unless properly prepared. One of the preparations is the institution of marriage."

Bro. Kwame went on to say that many young brothers thought they had to sleep with a girl to be a man. This, he said, was one of the biggest misconceptions of manhood. "It takes a real man to be committed, not to be a 'playa'. It takes a real man to wait until he's married. Sisters, what do you think?"

"Some of them boys write us notes, too, and call us all kinds of names!" retorted Kia.

"I know," replied Bro. Kwame. Hopefully none in here is doing that." He paused and looked at the brothers sternly. Then he continued, "...and remember, 'it's not what you're called, but what you answer to.' So don't answer to that mess. We also have to remember that we are not here just to make all the brothers look bad or make all the sisters look bad. We're here to lift brothers and sisters up."

"But what about them sisters who wear those tight clothes and short skirts? It's just like when you go to the store: if it's on display, it must be for sale," said Antonio.

"Many of those sisters don't know that they are sending a message to misguided brothers," said Bro. Kwame.

"Just because a sister is wearing something like that doesn't mean that she is trying to send that kind of message to other brothers," said Kia speaking up.

"Even though they may not be *intending* to send that kind of message, that is the way many brothers take it. I think some sisters dress in clothes like that because they want to gain attention. Sisters, you must understand that you are beautiful and attractive without exposing your body. Remember, your body is a temple," said Bro. Kwame.

"Now, I want you to carefully consider this saying," continued Bro. Kwame. *'Do not cast your pearls before swine.'*" He said it slowly and thoughtfully. "What do you think this saying means? What do the pearls represent?

"The pearls represent something valuable," said Jamilla. "Something worth a lot of money."

Good. You're right on track. Now what does the swine represent here?"

"Swine are pigs, aren't they?" asked Antonio.

"Are they considered to be clean or unclean, asked Bro. Kwame trying to draw the answers from the group.

"They're filthy," said Marcus. "They lay around in mud and each garbage.

"Yes. Yes. Now bring it all together," said Bro. Kwame, obviously pleased with the responses.

"What does this mean and how does it relate to our discussion?"

"Oh!" said Imani. The light bulb had just gone off in her head.

"Sis. Imani, do you have it?"

"Yes! Our bodies are very valuable...like the pearls. When we engage in sexual relations with many people or at the wrong time in our lives, it's like throwing ourselves into a hogpen and allowing ourselves to be wasted."

"Very well stated. Now how does that relate to how we should dress and present ourselves?"

"We should carry ourselves like we are valuable and precious and not expose ourselves to the world," said Jamilla.

"Great...and that goes for the brothers, too. I think you guys got the message," said Bro. Kwame proudly.

As the meeting drew to a close, the brothers vowed to be more respectful of sisters and the sisters vowed to be more respectful of themselves. The Sankofa Youth Group stood in a circle.

"Oh yeah…" said Bro. Kwame. "Don't forget we're responsible to do a presentation at the eleven o'clock service a week from Sunday. Kia and Imani will be representing us. Sisters, will you be ready to recite your poem?"

"Yes," said Imani.

"We'll be ready," added Kia.

"Alright," said Bro. Kwame. "Represent us well." As they stood in a circle hands held tightly, Bro. Kwame closed the meeting with a prayer.

II

"Imani, are you ready?" called Mrs. Johnson up the stairs.

"I'll be down in just a second," replied Imani. She was finishing getting dressed. It was Saturday morning and Imani was getting ready to go to the mall. She looked at herself in the mirror. She liked what she saw. She had brown eyes, high cheekbones, and a beautiful smile. Her braids were pulled back and partially wrapped with a piece of African cloth. She felt good about herself, but she wished more of the boys would notice her. She thought about dressing differently. The loose fitting jeans and t-shirt would not attract the attention she desired. Then she thought about the discussion at the Sankofa Youth Group. She was already pretty popular, but maybe if she dressed differently she would be more popular and be able to get the attention of some of the boys.

"Let's go, Imani. I have an appointment at five. If you and Kia want to go to the mall we have to hurry up," said Mrs. Johnson.

"Okay," said Imani. She finished looking in the mirror and ran down the stairs. They got in the car and picked up Kia. When they got to the mall, Mrs. Johnson said, "Okay, which shop do you ladies want to visit first?"

Imani and Kia looked at each other and giggled.

"What are you giggling about?" asked Mrs. Johnson.

"Mom, we'd rather go by ourselves. Can't we meet you somewhere later?"

"Ohhh. You don't want your friends to see you with 'dear old mom', huh?! That's okay," Mrs. Johnson said smiling. We'll meet back here in front of the ice cream shop in an hour. How's that?"

"That's cool," said Imani.

They walked off in opposite directions.

"Let's go to The Boutique," said Kia.

"Girl, that store is for older girls and women," said Imani.

"I saw a skirt in there that I wanna buy."

"The stuff they sell in there—I wouldn't wear it. Their skirts are cut too high and the other clothes are too tight," said Imani.

"I bet if you wore something from The Boutique you could get some attention from Jamal," said Kia smiling.

Imani's eyes got wide and she looked at Kia then quickly looked away embarrassed.

"See!" shouted Kia. "I knew you liked

him!"

"Shhh!," said Imani. "I do not."

"Yes you do! You two would look so cute together."

"It doesn't matter, he doesn't like me," said Imani whispering.

"That's what I'm trying to tell you. If you put on the right clothes, he'll notice you."

Kia took Imani by the hand and led her into The Boutique. Older teenage girls and women in their early twenties were browsing in the shop.

"Check this out," said Kia pointing to an outfit on display. It was a form fitting dress cut just above the thigh.

"Are you crazy?!" said Imani. "I would never wear that! My Mom and Dad would kill me if they saw me wear that!"

"They don't have to know," said Kia. Just wear your regular clothes and change into it when you get to school in the morning. Look, it's even on sale! Try it on."

Imani reluctantly went to the dressing room. When she had the dress on, she peeked out of the dressing room door.

"Well," said Kia. "Let's see."

Kia smiled as Imani stepped out.

"That's it! He'll love it," said Kia.

Imani quickly changed back into her

clothes and Kia took the dress to the counter. Imani paid the bill and they walked out of the shop.

"I can't believe I let you talk me into this... if my Mom and Dad find out..."

"They won't find out unless you tell them." said Kia. "Now let's go find you some earrings to match the outfit.

The two girls came back to the ice cream shop where they were supposed to meet Mrs. Johnson. Kia was holding the bag with the dress. When Mrs. Johnson saw them she looked down at her watch.

"Not bad, ladies. You're right on time. What did you get."

Imani froze.

"I just got a blouse and some earrings, Mrs. Johnson," said Kia.

"Well, are you two ready to go?"

"Yes," said Imani in an anxious voice.

*J*mani stood in front of the mirror holding her new dress in front of her. She was trying to envision herself in it. She was trying to picture Jamal's reaction when he would see her in it.

"I wonder if he'll like it," she thought to herself.

She didn't like being dishonest with her parents and up until now, she never had a reason to be dishonest. She was a good student and rarely got into any trouble. She took pride in these things and had always enjoyed shopping with her mother. They had a great relationship and she felt like she could talk to her about just about anything. She had always been Daddy's little girl. But now she was a teenager and she felt the need to show that she was maturing.

On Monday morning, Imani dressed in a sweatsuit and sneakers. When she got on the bus she saw Kia.

"Well?!" said Kia.

"Well, what?!" replied Imani.

"Did you bring the dress?"

Imani opened her backpack just enough for Kia to see the dress. When they got to school, they went into the restroom and changed. "Oh nooo!" cried Imani.

"What's wrong?" said Kia.

"I forgot to bring some shoes. I can't wear these gym shoes."

"I guess I have to think of everything," said Kia. Then she reached into her book bag and pulled out a pair of high-heeled sandals.

"I can't where those! I'm not allowed to wear heels yet."

Kia just looked at her as if to say, "You're

not supposed to be wearing the dress either, so you might as well go for it."

Imani couldn't stand the heat of the glare that Kia put on her. She snatched the sandals from Kia and put them on. "I don't even know how to walk in these things," she mumbled.

She took a deep breath and then walked, as best she could, out of the restroom. As she walked down the hall towards homeroom, she could see boys turning around and taking notice. She tried to walk naturally in the heels. There were whispers of surprise. Then she saw Jamal. Her heart started pounding. He walked up to her and said, "Hey, Imani."

"Hi," she said looking down shyly.

"You look nice today," he said looking her up and down from head to toe.

"Thanks," she said. By now her heart was racing. She couldn't believe that he actually noticed her. It worked.

"I have to go to homeroom, but I'll see you later," said Jamal.

"Okay."

She went to her homeroom class and took her seat. Marcus walked in.

"Hey Imani. I have a note for you."

He handed her a note. She opened it and it read:

"Will you go with me? Check yes or no. Love, Jamal."

Imani's heart raced. Her head was in the clouds.

"Imani?!" called Mrs. Ashanti.

Imani was so engrossed in the note that she didn't even hear her teacher call her.

"Imani?!" called Mrs. Ashanti again.

"Oh…yes, ma'am?

"Come here for a moment."

Imani went to up to Mrs. Ashanti's desk.

"Imani, do your parents know what you wore that to school today?"

Uhh…I…uhh," Imani stumbled over her words. Lying did not come easy to her. Her parents had taught her that nothing was worth lying for and she had always taken that to heart. Now she was in too deep and she didn't know what to say.

"That dress is awefully tight, wouldn't you say?" said Mrs. Ashanti. Let's go call your mother and see if she can bring you some other clothes to wear.

Imani's heart raced again, but his time for a different reason. She was about to be exposed. How would she explain?

III

She what?!" said Mrs. Johnson almost dropping the phone in shock and disbelief.

"She was wearing a dress that is against the dress code," said Mrs. Ashanti.

"I don't understand," said Mrs. Johnson still confused. "When she left the house this morning, she was wearing a sweatsuit. Can you describe this dress?"

"Well..." said Mrs. Ashanti, trying to be tactful. "...all I can say is that the top was cut low, the hem was much too high, and the whole thing was much too tight."

"That just doesn't sound like Imani," Mrs. Johnson thought out loud.

"You're exactly right," said Mrs. Ashanti. As soon as I saw her in it, I figured that you probably didn't know about it."

"Well where would she get something like that? We don't buy her clothes like that."

"Some of the girls have been leaving home dressed according to the dress code, but then when they get to school, they go into the restroom and change. Several girls have been sent home for repeated violations."

"She knows better than to do that. I can't believe she did this!"

"I know it's not like her. We have been trying to work with the young ladies about respecting themselves and carrying themselves with respect. To be honest, Mrs. Johnson, I think she was trying to impress some boy."

"Is that right?! Well we're going to get this straight immediately, before it goes any further. Thank you so much for calling and letting me know."

"Certainly," said Mrs. Ashanti. "I sent her back to the restroom to change into her sweatsuit."

"I will certainly be having *more* than just a talk with her this afternoon."

Seventh period was going by too quickly. Imani wished that it could last forever. She didn't know how she was going to face her mother when she got home, not to mention how she was going to face her father when he got home and heard the news. "Maybe I could plead 'temporary insanity,'" she thought to herself. "Why did I have listen to Kia?!"

After the seventh period bell rang, Imani stood at her locker, wasting time getting her things. She was trying to prepare mentally for the long walk home. Kia came up to her, smiling. When Imani saw Kia standing there, she rolled her eyes and turned around. Kia, still smiling said, "Welllll?!"

"Well what?!" said Imani in an exasperated tone.

"I saw Jamal checking you out! Did he ask you to go with him?"

"Yeah," said Imani smugly as she took her math book out and slammed the locker.

"That's great! It worked...what's wrong?"

Imani looked Kia in the eye. "Mrs. Ashanti called my mother and told her what I had on. Why did you make me wear that stupid dress? Even if Jamal does like me, I'll never be able to see him. I'm gonna be on punishment for the rest of my life!"

Kia, looked away. "It's not so bad...I mean, you accomplished your goal."

"My goal wasn't to lie to my parents! It's all your fault!"

"Hey, I didn't make you do anything you didn't want to do. I didn't make you put on that dress! "

Imani turned away and stormed off down the hall out the front doors of the school.

What in the world were you thinking, Imani?!" demanded Mrs. Johnson.

"It was Kia's fault," cried Imani trying to defend her own honor. "She was the one who got the dress."

"Did Kia tie you down and make you wear that dress?! That's a weak excuse and you're not a weak person, Imani." Mrs. Johnson's eyes were narrow and she was visibly angry. All Imani could do was hold her head down in shame. She couldn't even look her mother in the eye.

"I took time to take you two to the mall and this is what you buy behind my back?!" She yelled shaking the dress in front of Imani.

"I'm sorry I lied, Mom," said Imani through tears.

"Imani, you do so well in school, said Mrs. Johnson more calmly. "You always make me proud. It's not very often that I get upset with you. I'm more *disappointed* at you than I am angry. I know your father is going to have a lot to say about this, too."

For Imani that was the knock-out punch. She always tried so hard to please her parents and make them proud. Now she had not only disappointed them, she had disappointed *herself*.

IV

There was a knock on the door. Imani, with a solemn look on her face, was finishing her homework when the door to her room opened. As she looked up to see her father, she knew that this was perhaps the final stage of her humiliation. She looked down. What would he say? What would *she* say? She couldn't really tell what kind of mood he was in. All she could do was hold her breath and hope for the best.

"How are you feeling, Imani? he asked.

She looked up briefly to see a look of concern on her father's face. "Not good," she replied.

"Why, what's wrong?" he asked.

"It wasn't my fault, Daddy!" she cried. "I can explain..."

"Wait a minute. Slow down. I heard that something happened at school today. Now I want hear your version of what happened. Slow down and explain carefully."

Imani let out a deep sigh. She wanted to make sure she explained the story completely and correctly. She felt so misunderstood. But then again, she did *lie*. How would she explain this. She had always been honest with her parents. She knew that honesty would definitely be the best policy now, too, especially at this point.

"Daddy, I did something I shouldn't have."

"And what's that?" he replied.

"I wore a dress that was against the dress code."

"Describe the dress."

"Well...it was red...it was a little short...and a little tight."

"What do you mean 'a little?'"

"I shouldn't have worn it."

"Even if it was not against your school's dress code, would it have been against your mother's and my dress code?"

"Yes," she said looking down.

"Where did you get this dress from anyway?"

"From Kia...but...I bought it while we were at the mall."

"Well, I guess this is the most important question. *Why* did you do it. If you knew it wasn't right, why did you do it?"

Imani looked away too embarrassed to respond.

"Come on," said Mr. Johnson. There must be a good reason why you would break *our* rules *and* the school rules."

"I wanted someone to notice me," she said quietly as she buried her face in her hands."

"Let me get this straight. You had to disobey your parents and the school rules to impress a boy? Do you think he was worth it?

"Not now."

"What do you mean *not now*?"

"I mean...I didn't think it all the way through before I did it."

"Nooow we're getting somewhere!" said Mr. Johnson. "If someone saw you in this dress, what would be the first thing they would think about?"

Imani, still embarrassed, just looked down. "He just doesn't understand," she thought to herself.

"I know what you're thinking," said Mr. Johnson. "You're thinking I don't understand because I'm a guy...and that's precisely why I *do* understand. I used to be a boy once, you know." Imani, if you put your body on display, you're asking a young man to measure you according to your body rather than by your mind and spirit."

"I know," said Imani.

"I know you know, because we have discussed this before. That's why I'm surprised that you did this. But hopefully it will be a learning experience. Take out your Scriptures."

Imani reached over to the corner of her desk and slid her Bible to the center of the desk over her notebook.

"Turn to Proverbs 31:10 and read it out loud."

Imani found the Scripture and began reading, "'Who can find a virtuous woman? For her price is far above rubies.'"

"What is a 'virtuous woman'?" asked Mr. Johnson.

"A woman who carries herself with respect, speaks and acts intelligently, and dresses appropriately."

"Right. Why do you think the writer asks the question 'who can find a virtuous woman'?

"Because a lot of sisters don't carry themselves that way."

"Precisely. *You* are a virtuous young woman, Imani. Some sisters who are lost have not been raised to be virtuous, and so they sell themesleves short. But you *have* been raised to be virtuous. You know the truth."

"Daddy, it won't happen, again. I promise," pleaded Imani.

"Now jump down to verse 25. Read that."

"She is clothed with strength and dignity," read Imani.

"It sounds like, today, your clothes were weakness and low self-esteem instead of strength and dignity.

Imani didn't know what to say. She knew her father was right. She knew that normally, she would never have worn clothes like that. She did it only because she thought it might get Jamal's attention.

"I'm sorry, Daddy."

"Okay." He looked at her for a moment to gauge whether she was serious about her apology. When he saw that she was, he said, "Let's pray."

He took her hand and they both bowed their heads.

"Dear Lord, thank you for all of your blessings. You have blessed our family in many ways. You have provided food for our table, clothes for our backs, and a roof over our heads. You have even provided above and beyond our needs. We thank you for being so good to us. We even thank you for what happened this afternoon. Somehow there is a lesson to be learned in the midst of this. I pray for your continued guidance in all of our lives, especially in Imani's. Let your peace, providence and protection be upon her at all times. Help her to understand her purpose in this life and have the courage to complete it. Lord, my little girl is growing up. Please help her to be all you intended for a Woman to be. We ask these and all prayers in your Holy and Righteous name. Amen."

After finishing the prayer, Mr. Johnson got up and headed toward the door.

"You'd better start getting ready for bed soon."

"Okay...umm...Daddy?

"Yes."

"Why didn't you yell at me?"

"Your mother told me that *she* handled that part this time. We both figured yelling wasn't what you needed right now."

"She was right," said Imani with half of a smile.

"You're still on punishment for three weeks," said Mr. Johnson with a smile as he closed the door.

V

The night air rushed a cool breeze into Imani's room as she opened the window. She put her books in her book bag, turned out the light and got in the bed. The night air was cooler than she had thought when she raised the window. Imani pulled the covers up over her shoulder and closed her eyes. After a few minutes, the cold still chilled her through the covers.

She decided she would get up and close the window. Her mind made the decision, but her body did not respond. She tried to get up, but could not move. Try as she might, she could not seem to move a muscle in her body. As she tried to open her eyes to look around, her eyelids refused to cooperate, as well. She heard the wind whistle as it continued to move in and out of her window.

The wind grew louder. A loud rushing sound filled the air. Imani couldn't understand why she couldn't move. But it was the sound of the rushing wind getting louder and louder that began to frighten her even more. She felt something begin to pull on her—not pull on her body, but pull on her soul. Whatever seemed to be pulling her was relentless. It seemed to be related to the increasing power of the rushing wind. It would not let go.

With her eyes still closed and unable to move, Imani felt helpless. At the peak moment of her sense of helplessness she began to see shades of brown replace the darkness. The brown turned lighter until it was the color of sand. The rushing wind continued.

All of a sudden she found herself standing in the midst of a violent sandstorm. Even though she could now open her eyes, she couldn't keep them open. The wind blew relentlessly and sand got into her eyes. She put her hand up over her face and then tried to use her arm to shield her from the sand. She couldn't even see where she was going, but instinct told her to walk to try to find cover. Again, however, she felt helpless. Where was she? What should she do? Where could she find shelter?

"Over here," a faceless voice cried out.

Imani looked up and squinted her eyes just enough to see the silhouette of a woman. She was standing up and didn't seem to be the least bit affected by the wind or the sand.

"Give me your hand!" the woman cried.

Imani, hunched over still with her arm over her face and held out her hand. The woman grabbed her hand.

"Stand up straight and open your eyes," said the woman.

"But I can't see," cried Imani still afraid. "The sand gets into my eyes."

"Stand up and open your eyes," the woman repeated, this time in a more demanding tone. It was as if she was calling forth a power or untapped strength within Imani.

Imani slowly opened her eyes and stood up straight. As she did, the woman stretched forth her hands. The winds and the sands subsided. Imani was stunned but very relieved. She shook the sand from her hair.

"Where am I?" she asked.

"At the crossroads of your destiny," replied the woman.

"Huh?" replied Imani.

It was now, after shaking the sand from her head and bringing her eyes back into focus, that she could now see the woman's face and body. She was tall and stately. She had on a colorful robe. It had all the colors of the rainbow in it. It shimmered in the light of the sun. There was an intricately embroidered pattern on the robe, as well. Her neck and her wrists were covered regally with gold bands. The robe covered her from her neck to the ground. Imani could not see the woman's shoes or feet.

"I am your Ancestral Guide. My name is Ma'at."

"My name is Imani," said Imani extending her hand.

"I know who you are," said Ma'at, taking her hand firmly. "I know *exactly* who you are. You have been brought here to be reminded of *who you are*."

As she held Imani's hand firmly, a powerful energy was transmitted through the palm of her hand into Imani's. Imani felt it. It was almost like electricity. Imani pulled her hand back. She felt overwhelmed by the presence and power of Ma'at.

"There is no need to be afraid, Imani," said Ma'at in a caring voice. "The powerful energy you feel that is a part of my presence is also a part of your presence. I only represent the true power you have within. Don't be afraid to embrace your true power."

Imani just looked at her inquisitively.

"There are many things you must learn here before leaving. Come, we must go," said Ma'at walking toward her and pointing to something behind her.

When Imani turned around she saw a gigantic stone structure. It looked like it must have been a temple or learning center of some sort. As they walked toward the temple, Ma'at produced a scroll from her robe.

"Here," she said. Open and read."

Imani opened the scroll. It had all sorts of colorful symbols on it.

"I can't read this," said Imani.

Sure you can. All that you need to read that writing is within you. Look at it again and concentrate."

As Imani weighed the words of Ma'at in her mind, she looked down at the scroll again trying to focus. Amazingly, the longer she looked and concentrated, the more the symbols became recognizable. Somehow she began to understand what they said.

"These are the sacred writings which hold the truth of the ages," read Imani. "Follow each of these principles. Guard this wisdom by living a virtuous life..."

"So what are the principles?" asked Imani. "This is the only piece of paper in the scroll."

"Come," said Ma'at. The rest has been written on the walls of the temple.

As they walked through the doors of the temple, Imani noticed the huge stone blocks which made up the temple. She looked up to see a gigantic arch and columns along a wide center isle. On the walls she saw more of the colorful sacred writings. Her mouth opened with wonder at the awesome appearance of such an incredible sight. Ma'at led her to one of the walls.

"The first principle is *Truth*," said Ma'at.

"That sounds simple enough," said Imani. "There's nothin' real deep about that."

"Was it that simple when you lied to your parents about the dress."

Imani looked with both amazement and embarrassment.

"But…"

"How did I know that?" said Ma'at reading Imani's mind. "I know many things, Imani."

"You're right," said Imani shamefully. "It wasn't so easy."

"The Creator shaped and fashioned you in *Truth*. Your brain has over 14 billion brain cells. Each cell was created in *Truth*, to learn Truth, to know Truth, and live by the Truth. Every time you tell a lie or pass on a lie, it diminishes the capacity of your brain to accept truth."

"So every time I tell a lie, it makes it harder for me to understand the Truth?" asked Imani.

"Not only that," said Ma'at. "It makes it more difficult for you to live by the Truth. You see, Imani, if you live your life based on a lie, it is like building a house on the sands that were once in your eye. Your life will fall apart just like the house would. Some people's lives are tangled up in a web of lies."

"I don't lie very often," said Imani. She recognized the foolishness of her words as soon as they came out of her mouth.

"Anytime a lie is told, a bigger lie has to be told to cover it up and then another and so on and so on. Imani, if you don't understand this first principle, none of the others will make sense."

Now Imani was beginning to understand. The first lie that she told was when she and Kia got the dress. Then she lied by leaving the house dressed one way and changing when she got to school.

"I can see that you're beginning to understand. Lying clouds your judgement the way the sands clouded your vision earlier," said Ma'at.

"So what's the second principle?" asked Imani.

"Look over here," said Ma'at, beckoning her to a different wall in the temple. It was at this point that Imani noticed other people studying the writings on the walls.

"The second principle is *Justice*," said Ma'at.

"What does that have to do with me?" asked Imani. "I mean, I know at one time Black people didn't always receive justice in America and other places in the world, but..."

"You have just shown that you know very little about the second principle. Justice is the right consequence or outcome for every action."

"My Daddy said I'm on punishment for three weeks. That's not fair...that's not justice," complained Imani.

"Are you sure that's not justice?"

"Well..." she began to rethink her conclusion. "I did lie and go against my parents' rules and the school rules."

"Exactly. So your parents have done a fine job of using this second principle with you."

"But what about how Black people suffered for so long under slavery and all the other things that were done to us as a people? It seems like Whites never received proper justice."

"You're very right. It may 'seem' like they haven't received justice. However, nothing escapes the eyes of the Creator or the Universal Laws which the Creator put in place. Though it may appear that justice has been denied, justice has been at work all the while. Don't be fooled. Whatever you sow is what you reap. The land that you live in today is suffering greatly from the wrongs of the past. America was founded on violence toward Natives and Africans. Now the violence has come back around and is infecting the whole country in ways which seem uncontrollable."

"Unfortunately," said Imani, "it's affecting Black people the most, it seems. There's so much violence in our communities."

"You must live by the principles that I teach you. If you do, you will be able to help restore the peace, not only to Blacks and not only to Whites...but you will be able to restore peace to the whole world."

"What do you mean *I* will restore the peace? I can't do that."

"Imani, you still have yet to recognize the true power you have within. Everyone has this power, but few tap into it. When you tap into it, nothing will be beyond your reach. Absolutely nothing."

"How do I tap into this power?"

"Well, that leads to the third principle; it is *Righteousness*. If you live your life based on truth and always do your best to do what is right, and stand up for what is right...these are the keys which will unlock the power within."

"But what about all the other people in the world who choose to do wrong over right? I usually try to do the right thing...all the things my parents taught me. But it seems like more people want to do the wrong thing these days."

"Imani, in truth, there are actually more people who want to do the right things. A lot of people could go either way. Most people get swayed in the wrong direction, though. One of your leaders, a very wise man, once said, 'it's not that there are so many bad people in the world; it's just that the good people won't stand up.'"

"Yeah, but how do I change any of that? I'm just a young girl."

"Another wise one said, 'you must *be* the change you want to see in the world.' If you just live your life the way life ought to be lived, it will speak louder than any words you could put together. The energy of Righteousness in your life will begin to attract other like-minded brothers and sisters who will aid in the cause. The power of Righteousness is as strong as what you felt when I shook your hand. It can transform the world."

"It's hard to imagine myself making that kind of difference in the world," Imani thought out loud.

"You *must* spend some time imagining these things about yourself because whatever you think you can do is what you *will* do," replied Ma'at.

Imani looked off in the distance pondering what Ma'at said.

"Come now," said Ma'at. "We have more lessons to learn."

Ma'at led Imani out of the back door of the temple into a courtyard. It was lined with collossal pillars of stone. They walked for some time in silence until they came to the end of the stone pathway. They looked out over a field on the edge of the city.

"The next principle is *Reciprocity,*" said Ma'at.

"What is that? I've at least heard the other words before even if I didn't know everything they meant. But I've never even heard that word before."

"Though you may not have heard the word before...its meaning is quite simple and I know you are familiar with it: "What goes around..."

"...comes around," said Imani completing the sentence for her.

"Precisely," said Ma'at. Now let me ask you a question. Ma'at produced an apple seed and held it up between her index finger and thumb. "What would happen if I planted this seed in the soil?"

"It would grow an apple tree and the tree would produce apples," replied Imani.

"But what if I wanted mangoes instead of apples?"

"Then you need a mango seed. You can't plant an apple seed and expect mangoes to grow."

"It sounds silly to plant one thing and expect another, doesn't it?" asked Ma'at.

Imani nodded her head.

"But did you know people do it every day? People plant *hate* and expect *love* in return; they plant *violence* and somehow expect *peace* in return; they plant *disrespect* and somehow expect *respect* in return. It doesn't make sense does it?"

"Not at all," said Imani.

"Whatever you do, it will always come back to you. If you say or do something positive, it will always come back to you—mind you, it may not come when you expect it, but it will always come right on time. If you say or do something negative, it will always come back. Even when you think no one saw you or no one knows, this universal law of cause and effect kicks in. It is the principle of Reciprocity."

"That's going to make me think a little more carefully about what I do. The truth is, I didn't think *at all* before I did what I did. Before I knew it, I was in too deep. I was just...I just acted stupid"

"The things that I teach you are part of a life-long struggle. It is not easy, but you can gain mastery over these laws of the universe and use them to help yourself and others.

"I appreciate all these things you are teaching me, but how am I going to remember all this?"

"What I'm teaching you, you won't be able to forget even if you *want* to forget. When you stray from what I teach you, my words will come back to you; you will have constant reminders.

Imani was almost sorry she asked the question. She was starting to feel the burden of having been introduced to this higher knowledge and insight.

"No one could really blame you if you were never taught the truth. But when you have been taught the truth, you have a responsibility to act on it. To whom much is given..."

"...much is expected!" said Imani completing the sentence. "My Daddy always tells me that."

"Your father sounds like a very wise person," replied Ma'at. "Now we must go to Giza to learn of the next principle. But first let me introduce you to a very wise man who can give you some insight into it."

VI

ust then, Imani spotted a man walking toward them from inside the temple. He had on a long robe-like garment similar to Ma'at's. His head was shaved and his skin was velvety black and smooth. He had some kind of light or glow about his head. To Imani, he had the appearance of a monk. He looked like he knew something that Imani wanted to know. Intuitively, she knew he was was going to share something with her and she could not take her eyes off of him. He walked in slow measured strides, however, he looked more like he was gliding than walking. Though at first he appeared to be quite a distance from them, it was no time before he had reached Imani and Ma'at.

"Hotep, Bro. Tehuti," said Ma'at.

"Peace be unto you, as well, Sis. Ma'at." Tehuti had his hands folded in front of himself and bowed to Ma'at.

"I have a young sister seeking wisdom and I knew you would be able to provide her insight on some of the lessons that I am sharing with her."

Tehuti turned to Imani and greeted her

in the same fashion that he greeted Ma'at.

"Peace be unto you, young sister."

"Peace be to you, too, sir," said Imani.

"Imani, Bro. Tehuti is a scribe. He copies the holy writings called the *medu neter*. He is also the Messenger among us. He brings us the proper understanding of the wisdom of the sacred writings," said Ma'at.

Tehuti looked at Imani intently, but said nothing. Imani was transfixed by his gaze. She was unable to speak. He continued to look at her for a moment, then he spoke.

"Young sister, the lips of wisdom are closed except to the ears of understanding. Are your ears ready to receive the wisdom of the Ancestors?"

Imani wanted very badly to say yes, but she wasn't sure if she could. She didn't know if she was ready to receive the wisdom he was going to share. She began to doubt herself. She just didn't know how to respond.

It was as if Tehuti was reading her every thought. Still looking into Imani's eyes very intently, he said, "your heart has been made pure by the things Ma'at has shared with you. You are more ready than you think you are. Come, let us go to Giza."

They walked back into the temple, through to the front and out the doors. Off in the distance she saw the peaks of the three pyramids of Giza. She began to feel herself gliding along as she had seen Ma'at and Tehuti do earlier. Before she knew it, she found herself standing in front of the Great Pyramid.

It was sparkling white and gleaming in the sun. It wasn't like pictures she had seen in books with brown crumbling blocks. There was an incredible capstone on top that was pure gold.

"This is incredible," said Imani in awe of the Seventh Wonder of the World. "It's different than the pictures I've seen."

"Years before the modern pictures of the pyramids, they looked like what you see right now. They were encased in polished white limestone. Years later, when the Kingdom of Kemet began to fall, Arab thieves came and chipped away all of the limestone and took the capstone of gold. They also burrowed their way inside to steal the many treasures within."

"What does the pyramid have to do with the next principle? asked Imani.

"Like the thieves who chipped away the precious limestone, ignorance chipped away at your self-esteem and caused you to disobey your parents. Like the thieves who burrowed their way inside the pyramid, falsehood has burrowed its way into Truth and attempted to steal the riches within. Imani, each of us is a walking buried treasure.   But you must dig deep to find the treasure within."

"The principle that Sis. Ma'at has asked me to share with you is the principle of *Balance*," said Tehuti.

"Balance?" asked Imani. You mean like standing up straight without falling?"

"No," said Tehuti. "It's a little deeper than that. How many sides does a pyramid have?"

"Three," said Imani proudly as if she had just answered a million-dollar question.

"No young sister. A triangle has three sides. How many does a pyramid have?

"Oh," said Imani realizing her mistake. "A pyramid has four sides."

"Correct. Our People always had a deeper meaning in everything they did, even in the buildings they constructed. Each side of this pyramid represents a part of your nature."

"A part of my nature?" said Imani. "I don't understand."

"Well," said Tehuti, "there is your spiritual side, your mental side, your emotional side, and your physical side. Perhaps you will understand better from a different vantage point."

With that he took Imani and Ma'at by the hand and began walking on the air.

"Wait!" cried Imani. She was gripped

with fear as she tried to pull away. Ma'at looked over at her. In a very calm and reassuring voice, Ma'at said, "Imani, you are protected; all you have to do is believe."

Once again, Ma'at's words penetrated her fears. She remembered back to when she was four years old and asked her mother what her name meant. "Your name means 'faith', sweetheart. Always believe in God and *yourself*. That's why we named you *Imani*." Her mother's words were like surround- sound stereo in her mind. Imani began to relax as they stepped up higher and higher on the air. She no longer resisted. Once relaxed, she marveled at the view of everything she could see from hundreds of feet above the ground.

Within seconds they found themselves standing atop the magnificent Great Pyramid. Imani took a deep breath and looked around in all four directions. The view was so breathtaking that she was speechless.

"Imani," said Tehuti, "this pyramid represents a stairway to Heaven. If you can bring the spiritual, mental, and emotional parts of yourself together in complete *Balance* with your physical self, it will be as if you are walking up the stairway to Heaven. The incredible and exhilarating feeling that you felt when you got to the top will be the feeling you wake up with every morning. But you must balance your life."

"So…" thought Imani, "if I live my life by committing myself to what you two have taught me, you're saying I can find happiness on earth."

"Yes," said Tehuti. But human beings make this so much more complicated than it has to be. It is only a matter of focusing all of our spiritual and mental energy to produce the proper emotions and physical environment. What we focus on is what we're moving toward."

"Momma always says that Sunday is not the only day to get right with God. She said too many people leave church on Sunday and then do the same wrongs over and over throughout the week," said Imani. "She said we should try to live by our faith every day."

"It sounds as if your mother is spiritually in balance. However, there are far too many people that are *out of balance*," said Tehuti. "Many people do not have parents who are directing them in the right way."

"I guess I'm kinda lucky then," said Imani. My parents always pray with me and teach me the right things."

"That's not luck," said Ma'at. "That is a blessing from the Most High. You should give thanks for it every day."

With that, she took Tehuti and Imani's

hand and they glided down to the base of the pyramid.

"I must be going, Sisters," said Tehuti.

"Thank you for sharing your knowledge with me," said Imani.

"Use it well, young Sister...and balance the Scales."

Imani turned to Ma'at and asked, "What does he mean *'balance the scales'*?"

As she turned around to look back in Tehuti's direction, he was gone. When she turned back to Ma'at she saw a marble table standing between them. On top of the marble table was a solid gold set of scales. These scales were like none she had ever seen before. They were shaped like a symbol. She recognized the symbol, but she could not remember what it was.

"I've seen that symbol before," said Imani. "My mother always wears a necklace with that symbol on it. What does it mean?"

"These scales are in the shape of an ankh," replied Ma'at. "It is the ancient symbol of life everlasting. Too many people are bringing forth death, but if you can balance these scales, you will bring forth life through your example to others."

Ma'at placed a feather on one side of the Scales. She then knelt down and picked up

several pebbles in her hand and placed them on
one end of the scale. The Scales began to tilt
due to the imbalance of the pebbles being
weighed against the feather.

"This represents your heart," said Ma'at
pointing to the feather. "These represent wrong
actions you have done in your lifetime," she
said pointing to the pebbles. "Your task is to
decrease the number of wrongs you do until you
can balance the Scales through your Righteousness. Most people's hearts are weighed down
with poor decisions and wrongdoing. Imani,
you must balance the Scales by living the principles which we teach you here."

Imani nodded focusing intently on the
Scales. She then reached forth her hand and
began removing the pebbles one by one until
there were no more. The Scales began to balance and all that remained on one side was the
weightless feather.

"I will balance the Scales by the way I
live my life," said Imani. She spoke in such a
matter-of-fact tone that she even surprised herself. She had an acute sense of knowing that
she would keep her promise, even though she
might make some mistakes along the way.

"Now you are beginning to see the light,"
said Ma'at smiling a beautiful, peaceful smile.
" We have but two principles left."

Imani felt somehow different; she felt as though she were growing, but not physically. Something was happening on the inside that she couldn't quite pinpoint. But she knew she would be forever changed by this experience.

Look over there," said Ma'at. Imani looked in the direction that Ma'at pointed. She looked off into the distance of the western sky. She saw the sun sitting high in the sky . In a matter of seconds, it began to descend behind the horizon. It was like a sunset happening all at once. Just as quickly, the sky was filled with darkness and tiny bright flickering stars.

"This is beautiful," she said looking up at the clear black sky.

"There is a lesson in the blackness," replied Ma'at. "It is the principle of *Order*."

"You mean there is Order throughout the Universe?" asked Imani.

"Yes," said Ma'at. "But not only that. If my dear friend Bro. Tehuti was still here he would tell you 'as above, so below.'"

"What does that mean?"

"Are you familiar with constellations, Imani?"

"Yes Ma'am. We learned all about them in Mrs. Ashanti's class. My father is a star gazer, too. I learned how to identify the Big Dipper and the Little Dipper," said Imani, pointing up to the heavens. "I can see the North Star...and there's Orion the Hunter...see his belt?"

"Your Ancestors were able to chart these patterns in the heavens. They noticed that the Most High created the Universe with order. Our lives must reflect that same Universal Order on earth. Remember, 'as above, so below.' But many people's lives are in disorder because they have not followed the proper path. There are many whose lives are like the sandstorm I rescued you from. Their foolish choices are like the sands which blinded you from seeing clearly."

"I want to see things clearly in my life and help other people, too," said Imani.

"Then you must commit yourself to live your life in proper Order," said Ma'at. One person whose life is in *disorder* can bring disorder to a whole family, community, society, nation, and so on. But, a person who lives a life in Universal Order can have the same effect, only in a positive way. Regardless of what anyone else is doing, Imani, live your life in order."

Imani took a deep breath and exhaled. It was as if she was breathing in the wisdom Ma'at had just shared. She looked around at the beautiful blackness of the sky out into the far reaches of the Universe.

"Whenever I look up at the sky and see all those stars and distant galaxies, I always wonder what else is out there," said Imani.

"The sacred writings tell us 'the Universe is like a book; anyone who learns the language can read the knowledge of history and humanity.' Imani, as vast as the Universe is around you, it can never compare to the vastness of the Universe *within*. Just like there is more to be discovered out there in space. There is infinitely more to be discovered within."

As Imani pondered Ma'at's words, she heard a faint sound off in the distance. It was a beautiful melody. It sounded like a flute or some sort of wind instrument.

"What's that sound?" asked Imani.

Ma'at did not reply. She simply listened thoughtfully to the music for a moment, then smiled.

"Where is it coming from?" thought Imani aloud. "It sounds like it's coming from inside the pyramid. Can we go inside?"

"Certainly," said Ma'at.

They walked around to the entrance of the Great Pyramid. The melodic sound grew slightly louder, and more pronounced, though it was still faint. It echoed as the sound waves reflected off of the walls of the inner chambers in the pyramid. Ma'at led Imani through corridors and passageways. The sound grew louder and louder. Some of the corridors were narrow, some wide. Some were slanted going upward, some slanted going downward. All of them were dimly lit by candles on the wall every hundred feet or so. Each time Imani turned a corner or entered another corridor, she thought she would find the source of the music.

She was very anxious to see what this incredibly soothing sound was and who was producing it. The music was a magnet and she was like metal being drawn to it. Finally, they entered a large circular room and saw a man surrounded by a circle of candles sitting on the floor blowing a wooden flute. This was the man who was somehow able to blow life into this wooden instrument and produce the sound she treasured. Somehow he had opened new dimensions of peace, insight and understanding in Imani. It was as if the music added clarity to all the things Ma'at had taught her. She wanted to talk to him and express to him how beautiful his music was. She did not, however, want to interrupt him because he was not finished playing.

She wondered if he was going to stop and speak to her, but she soon realized that the only speaking he intended to do was through his flute. Ma'at silently summoned her to sit on the floor. Once seated, Imani looked around the large room. There were other doorways leading into the room, three others to be exact. She and Ma'at had entered through the east door.

Then, from the darkness of the west doorway, emerged a young boy. He looked to be about Imani's age. He had the same anxious and intrigued look on his face that Imani had. He took a seat on the floor; apparently he had been drawn to the music also. Then from another doorway emerged a young girl. Then came another boy from the other doorway. Imani noticed that the boys and girls who entered were from different ethnic backgrounds. She saw every nationality represented. Each child had on the native dress of his or her country of origin. Soon the room was filled with silent young people, entranced by the beauty of the melody coming from the simple wooden flute of the man in the center of the circle.

It was all such a beautiful and colorful sight to see all of the children dressed in their native garb. Imani closed her eyes and continued to drink in the melody of the flute and the peaceful ambiance. All the lessons from Ma'at and Tehuti ran slowly through her mind. She felt light as a feather. After relaxing in the midst of the melody, Imani opened her eyes and looked around the room again. Many of the young people had their eyes closed in meditation as she had. Then she did a double take. There was a girl over on the other side who looked like—it was *Kia!*

"You didn't think you were the only one, did you, Imani?" asked Ma'at in a whisper. Imani had a look of surprise on her face. "There are many others who have been brought here to learn, just as you. And there are many more we must bring here to reawaken their higher awareness." The flutist was concluding his musical masterpiece as Ma'at turned to the rest of the children.

"Children, you are Chosen," she said in a powerful voice. "You have just learned the wisdom of the ages and you have been re-introduced to the knowledge of the Universe. It has always been in you. Now it is time for you to come forth by day for the redemption of Humanity. No more hiding your intelligence, insight, and higher awareness in the darkness. You must let it be seen in the light.

"You have just learned the last principle of *Harmony* without anyone saying a word to you. When we all come together as one to deal truthfully and righteously with the problems of Humanity, we will do away with hunger, poverty, disunity, hatred, war and bloodshed. You are the leaders of this world revolution. Go and bring peace back to the Earth. Africa is the Motherland, the birthplace of Humanity, and the center of the world. Restore Mother Africa to her traditional greatness. Go then, to every land near and far and do the same. Let your life be so completely in tune with what you have learned here, that, like the melody, you will draw others to you. Resurrect the higher consciousness of your brothers and sisters around the globe. Shemhotep...walk in peace."

With that, the man began playing the flute again. The melody pulled on Imani's spirit and she felt certain that everyone else in the room must have felt the same incredible peace she did. This feeling was soon transformed into a sense of urgency—an urgency to get back to share what she had learned, to talk about what she had learned. No...wait...she couldn't just talk about it. Her Higher Self began to speak to her. She must simply *live* what she had learned. Like the man who did his talking by blowing the flute, Imani realized that she needn't talk about her experience, just *live* it, just *be* it. *Living it* would be all the talking she would need to do. She closed her eyes and bathed in the beauty of the melody. She floated up... up... out... off... far... away... back.

Imani woke to the wind blowing

through her window. The window was raised about six inches. The wind was not too cool, but just right, producing a soothing breeze.

"Live it...live it," was the message of the breeze. "Be it...be it," whispered the wind as she sat up in bed and wiped the last grain of sand from her eyes.

VII

$\mathcal{I}$mani took a seat in the empty fellowship hall of the church where the Sankofa Youth Group met. It was Sunday morning and Imani wanted to get in one more practice run of the poem that she and Kia were to recite in front of the whole congregation. The poem was Maya Angelou's "Still I Rise."

She went into the small restroom in the hall, turned on the light, and looked in the mirror. She looked at herself from head to toe. She wore a beautiful headwrap out of which her braids could be seen flowing from the back. She ran her hand along the cowry-shell necklace and noticed the matching bracelet which adorned her wrist. The matching cowry shell earrings dangled from her ears completing her accessories.

Her top was long and loose fitting. It was a beautiful African print. The long skirt of a purple African print matched the top and the headwrap and descended to her ankles. The black sandals she wore complemented the whole outfit. She remembered that her mother and father told her that she looked like a princess as they all left the house together that morning. Imani was proud of herself and knew that Ma'at would be, too. She turned out the light in the bathroom and sat alone at one of the tables in the fellowship hall.

She hadn't spoken to Kia since she saw her at her locker before leaving school Friday. Then, she had lashed out at Kia. But now she realized that it wasn't all Kia's fault. As a matter of fact, the bulk of the responsibility was on Imani to be able to withstand the pressure that Kia had put on her. Now there was tension between them and in a few minutes, they had to make a presentation in front of the whole church. She decided she would try to make amends with Kia by apologizing for yelling at her and blaming her for mistakes that she herself had made.

Just then, Kia walked in. Kia was adorned in a very colorful kente cloth outfit. It was cut much like Imani's. It had red, green, black, purple, orange, and yellow all in a magnificent pattern. The long top and skirt extended to her ankles, as well. Around her neck, Kia wore a golden ankh. It immediately drew Imani's attention and reminded her of the scales of Ma'at.

When she saw Imani, Kia lowered her eyes in embarrassment.

"Imani," she said, "I'm sorry I pressured

you into wearing that dress. I...I don't know what I was thinking...I mean...it goes against everything we've learned and everything we believe in."

Imani smiled a little. "I'm sorry for blaming you for everything. You were right on Friday. You didn't make me do anything that I didn't already want to do. I should have been strong enough to resist."

"We've been friends since kindergarten," said Kia. "We shouldn't let something like this ruin our friendship."

"I agree," said Imani. The two friends hugged each other.

"I like your dress," said Kia.

"Yours looks good, too. I bet you didn't find *that* at the Boutique." They smiled and laughed.

The door to the fellowship hall opened and in came Bro. Kwame.

"Oh, great! I see you two got here early to practice the poem. Alright now...make us look good. Remember, you're representing Sankofa Youth Group. Make it strong, sisters."

The rest of the young brothers and sisters of the group came into the fellowship hall. Bro. Kwame rounded them up into a circle and lifted up the group in prayer. In the middle of the prayer, he prayed that Imani and Kia would help to awaken some lost brothers and sisters when they recited their poem.

"Let everyone say together…" concluded Bro. Kwame.

"Amen!" they all said together in a strong unified voice.

℘astor Reed walked magestically to the pulpit as the choir was finishing a spirit-filled hymn. He seemed almost to be floating in his long white robe with the colorful African embroidery along the collar.

"Brothers and sisters, we are very proud of the young people here at our church," he intoned. "Oh I know you see young folks doing all sorts of things these days, but *all* of our young people haven't gone astray."

"Amen!" replied the attentive congregation.

"As a matter of fact, there are a lot of young people who are working hard to better themselves and are doing the right thing. We've got some young people here today like that who love the Lord. But before we bring them on, y'all give Bro. Kwame here a round of applause. It's one thing to talk about what our youth ought to be doing, but it's another thing to actually spend time with our youth…train them up in the way they should go...Bro. Kwame has been working hard with these young brothers and sisters."

"Amen" shouted the congregation with applause.

"So now we have two young sisters from our new Sankofa Youth Group who are going to bless us with a poem. Don't they look beautiful?! Y'all pray with young Sis. Kia and Sis. Imani. Give them a round of applause as they come up."

The congregation began to encourage Imani and Kia as they made their way to the pulpit. Imani spoke first in her best public speaking voice. She was careful to use standard English and speak clearly and articulately.

"We would like to present a poem to you from Dr. Maya Angelou. It is entitled "Still I Rise.""

"Alright," said someone in the congregation.

"We feel that this poem captures the essence of what it means to be a conscious and virtuous Woman of God."

The congregation applauded again.

"You may write me down in history with your bitter twisted lies..." said Kia with power and conviction.

"You may trod me in the very dirt, but

still, like dust, I rise!" said Imani.

The congregation was clearly impressed as the two young sisters continued. They didn't just recite the poem. They *presented* it. They didn't just memorize the poem, they had internalized it and knew it in their hearts. It truly showed as they went from verse to verse back and forth taking their turn at the microphone.

"Out of the huts of history's shame, I rise," intoned Kia.

"Up from a past that's rooted in pain, I rise; I'm a black ocean, leaping and wide, welling and swelling I bear in the tide." replied Imani. By this time the congregation was on its feet saying, "Go'head sisters!"

"Leaving behind nights of terror and fear, I rise."

"Into a daybreak that's wonderfully clear, I rise."

Nearing the end, Imani wanted to really bring the house down. Somehow, Kia sensed Imani's thoughts and raised it to the next level.

"Bringing the gifts that my Ancestors gave," said Imani with great conviction. As the words proceeded out of her mouth, a flash from her visitation by Ma'at, Tehuti, and the man with the flute ran across the stage of her mind. It was in this fleeting moment that Imani saw very clearly what her purpose was.

"I am the dream and the hope of the slave," said Kia with all the inner strength she could muster.

Then, they looked at each other and said in unison with the congregation joining in, "I RISE, I RISE, I RISE!"

The church thundered with applause from the standing ovation. There were many praises to the Lord for using these two young messengers to bring such a powerful message. But as the people continued to applaud, Imani joined in the applause. She wasn't applauding for herself, nor was she applauding for Kia, although Kia certainly deserved it. She was giving thanks for the powerful Spirit of God moving in, around, and through her. She applauded because time had stood still for a moment. And in that brief, yet timeless moment, Imani had found what few others do in this life. Imani had found *a reason for being*.

Daniel and the Djembe Drum

"Come on man…take a hit," said Johnny.

"Man you know Daniel ain't gonna do that," said Jerome.

The sun was bright as the trees were blooming. Heritage Park was a favorite hangout spot after school for Daniel and his friends. The grass was green, the pond sparkled with blue waters so clear you could see the fish swimming. There were tree-lined walkways all around the park. People could be seen walking their dogs, riding their bikes, jogging, or just sitting under the shady trees reading. Johnny, Jerome, and Daniel were off in a more secluded spot to hide from any adults or police who might be around.

"Man, y'all are stupid. Why do you smoke that stuff?" said Daniel.

"It feels good," said Jerome.

"It can't be *that* good," said Daniel. "That's why you fell asleep in Algebra. Smokin' that mess kills your brain cells."

"Man, shut up!" said Johnny. You always talkin' like a goodie goodie! Here, just take a hit and see for yourself," he said shoving the weed into Daniel's hand.

Daniel looked at the smoking cigarette and for a moment actually considered taking a puff despite the thoughtful warnings he had just given to his friends. Then he came back to his senses.

"Naw man, I can't do it!" said Daniel.

"See man...I keep tellin' you he ain't gonna do it, ever since he been studyin' that African stuff at the community center...he can't even hang with us no more!" said Jerome to Johnny.

"He's a punk," Johnny said laughing. "But you're still my boy...I ain't gonna keep messing with you about it."

"Come on, let's go," said Jerome.

"Wait a minute," said Johnny. Then he took a long drag on the cigarette, threw it to the ground and stepped on it to put it out. Daniel rolled his eyes and they all walked out from behind the bushes. They walked along the path beside the pond. The pond had clear blue water with ducks gliding peacefully. The still water reflected the light of the sun and the silhouette of the trees.

Off in the distance, Daniel heard a drum beating. It wasn't like the drums you would hear in modern bands. It was an African drum. He had heard this sound before when he was a little boy. He remembered hearing his father play in the basement when he returned home from work late at night.

"Do y'all hear that?" said Daniel.

"Hear what?" asked Johnny.

"Looks like you're the one hearing things and losing your mind and you didn't even smoke," said Jerome sarcastically.

"No...listen," said Daniel.

"Aw man...that's just a drum," said Johnny.

"I know," said Daniel. "I've always wanted to learn how to play the drum since my dad used to do it."

"Man, to play the drum, you gotta have rhythm," said Jerome.

"I got rhythm!" said Daniel.

"Oh yeah?" said Jerome. "It didn't look like you had rhythm at the party last Friday when you were dancing with Tameka and tripped and fell down!" Johnny and Jerome burst into laughter. Daniel couldn't help but laugh, too. The fact that Jerome was always joking him was what let him know that they were cool. Daniel appreciated the fact that Jerome had the peculiar ability to lighten up any situation, even an embarrassing one.

"Danny, we're going to the movies this Friday. You gonna roll with us?" asked Johnny.

"I can't...I told you guys we have the final ceremony for my Manhood Training."

"It's gonna take a lot more than a few classes to make you a man by Friday," said

Jerome laughing.

"You guys should come and check it out," said Daniel. "You might like it."

Johnny and Jerome just shook their heads no. They had already had this discussion with Daniel. Daniel had tried to get them to join the rites of passage.

"What's a rites of passage?" Johnny had asked him.

"It's a process where a boy becomes a man. You have to pass certain physical, mental, and spiritual tests to prove yourself."

"Nah...I'm already *the* man," Jerome had said poking out his chest.

Try as he might, Daniel had not been able to convince the guys to join. And why should they? Daniel himself hadn't actually wanted to do it. His mom and grandmother had made him do it.

As the boys continued to walk, off in the distance Daniel noticed a man sitting under a large oak tree. The branches of the oak stretched far and wide, the leaves fully formed and a radiant green, acted as sort of a natural umbrella from the bright rays of light dripping from the afternoon sun. The man sat in the shade on a small stool beating a drum.

From a distance, the man looked like he was wearing pajamas. As they drew closer on the path, Daniel noticed that he was not wearing pajamas, but a dashiki, wide-leg drummer pants, and leather sandals. The outfit had many colors, but was slightly faded. While at first the man appeared to be praying or maybe meditating with his eyes closed while playing the drum, his eyes were now open and he appeared to be looking in the direction of the three boys.

The path the boys were walking on led away from the oak tree where the man was drumming. It became apparent that the man was looking at Daniel.

"Yo man..." said Jerome leaning over to Daniel. "Let's go by the gym and play some ball?

"No," said Daniel. I gotta get home."

"C'mon man," said Johnny. "I won't beat you so bad this time," he said laughing.

"I gotta go home and see if my grandmother needs anything before I go anywhere."

"Alright man," said Jerome. We'll catch you later."

Johnny and Jerome continued on the path they were on and Daniel turned to the other sidewalk which led past the tree where the man was playing the drum. The man was still looking at him. But by this time, Daniel was almost entranced by the rhythmic beat the man was playing. It was as if it was opening up parts of his mind that had never been opened before.

Daniel wanted to speak to the man, but he didn't know what to say. Daniel was not in the habit of walking up to people he didn't know and striking up conversation. He tried to just walk by and look in the other direction.

"Peace be unto you, young brother," said the old man. His voice was magnetic, not loud, but it drew Daniel's complete attention. He had a thick accent, but Daniel could not tell where the old man must have been from. The old man hadn't stopped beating the drum, he only beat it more lightly so that the volume went down.

"Good afternoon, sir," said Daniel. He felt awkward. Should he stop to talk or keep on walking?

You must be wondering why I was looking at you while you were with your friends back there, huh?"

"Well...yeah," said Daniel. "Actually I was."

"Because...," said the old man, "...to whom much is given, much is required." Then he looked back down at his drum, closed his eyes and beat a loud drum roll.

It startled Daniel. He wanted to respond, but didn't know what to say. "What is this guy talking about?" he thought to himself. The man's eyes were still closed and he was focused on his own drumming. Daniel continued on the path until it led out of the park.

II

$\mathcal{I}$t was the final day of the rites of passage and Daniel was anxious. For nine months, he and eleven other young men were in Manhood Training at the Heritage Park Community Center. Daniel hadn't been able to hang out with Johnny and Jerome very often since he had been in the rites of passage.

Men from local churches and businesses in the community had come together to sponsor this manhood training program. Meetings were twice a week and the program was not easy.

"It's not supposed to be easy," Daniel remembered his grandmother saying when he complained about having to memorize and recite African proverbs. "Things that are worth having in life never come easy, but it makes you appreciate them. There are certain things that your mother and I can't teach you about being a man. So you're going to stay in this program and give it everything you've got."

"But none of my friends are in the rites of passage. I asked Jerome and Johnny to join me, but they didn't want to."

Sometimes you are called to a different path than your friends," said his grandmother. "They're just missing out and they'll regret it when they see what you've learned and how you've grown as a result of it."

Now Daniel was sitting on the front row of chairs reserved for the Twelve Initiates. They had bonded in a mighty way. They had studied together, worked together, trained together, played together, prayed together, and been transformed together.

The drum roll began. The beautiful sounds of African rhythms filled the air as the Elders took their seats on the platform. They had all marched in together in a procession. It was a meditational moment for Daniel and the rest of the Initiates. He began to think back to some of the activities that they had come through. He remembered the time they went camping over a weekend. The Twelve Initiates had been dropped off in the woods and were instructed to find their way back to camp before sundown. It was a frightening and potentially disastrous experience. All the Initiates had were their backpacks, inside of which was water, a compass, a camping knife, a flair, and a first aid kit. The Initiates had to overcome their fears, use team work, unity, and critical thinking skills to make it back to the camp safely. This they did, despite the fact that three almost got into a fight, one cried and wanted to give up, and two did not pack their backpacks with all of their supplies. But they learned some powerful lessons about life on the way.

Daniel then remembered the big football game that the Elders played against the Initiates. He had scored a touchdown with only a few minutes left, but then got scored on by one of the Elders on the last play of the game. It was a great game and everyone had fun. He thought about the early meetings on Saturday mornings at 6 am. "A man must rise with the sun and begin the day's work with the fullness of his strength and energy," the Elders had told him. The Elders were the men who were leading the rites of passage. They came from all walks of life. Some were businessmen, construction workers, teachers, doctors, janitors, and engineers. But they were all committed to making sure that the Initiates understood first hand the responsibilities of being a man.

Then there was the garden in which the young brothers learned to grow onions, cabbage, lettuce, turnip greens, tomatoes, and other vegetables. "We must learn how to grow our own food and be self-sufficient, the Initiates were told by the Elders. Have you noticed that none of the grocery stores in our community are owned by us? Why is that?" Then a discussion would ensue.

There was so much that Daniel had learned, he was glad that his grandmother didn't let him quit when the going got a little rough. There was so much he had learned about African history and culture, spirituality, and cooperative economics. There was so much he had learned about the Ancestors, the Elders, and the other Initiates. But most of all, there was so much he had learned about *himself*. He had learned to confront his fears, listen to his Higher Self within, work smart and hard, and he learned to look out for his fellow Initiates, by encouraging them and helping them. He had gained a sense of pride and commitment. He was intent on being a part of the solutions that the community needed rather than a part of the problem.

Behind Daniel sat his mother and his grandmother as well as the friends and family of all the other Initiates. Many had come out to see the Initiates be presented to the community as young men. He had somehow convinced Johnny and Jerome to come and they were seated in the rear checking out the scene.

"We'll be there," Jerome had said.

"Yeah, man," Johnny had said. "If it means that much to you." And it did mean that much to him. The three boys had been tight since elementary school. They had been in trouble together, gotten suspended together, even made the honor roll together when Johnny bet them that he was the smartest. They had been through thick and thin together. Daniel still regretted that they had not joined him in the rites of passage, but he appreciated that they had come to see him on his special day.

The presiding Elder, Bro. Kofi, walked to the podium and began to speak.

"Brothers and sisters, we have been called here today in the midst of the Most High and in the presence of our Ancestors to present these young men to the community. When they joined us nine months ago, they were boys. Now they are young men. Just as it takes a child nine months in its mother's womb to grow properly before it can be born, it takes time for a boy to be reborn into a man. Though there are many trials that lay ahead for these young men, they have shown that they have accepted the call to consciousness. But before we honor these young brothers, first we honor God and our Ancestors with the Libation Ceremony."

Bro. Kofi took a wooden cup with water, held it over a plant which was on a stand next to the podium.

"The Libation Ceremony is an opportunity for us to remember the trials and tribulations as well as the triumphs and victories of our Ancestors. During this time we give thanks for their contributions in building great civilizations as well as their commitment to our struggle for liberation since slavery and colonization. We call the names of the departed and then all say together 'ashe', meaning 'I agree.' We pour a drop of water into the plant because water represents life and we know that the spirits of our Ancestors live though they have departed in the flesh."

Bro. Kofi paused and held up the cup. "I pour libation for Imhotep, the African Father of Medicine."

"Ashe!" the audiece replied.

Another of the Elders rose and said, "I pour libation for Queen Nzingha."

"Ashe!"

I pour libation for Sojourner Truth," said another of the Elders.

"Ashe!"

Bro. Kofi opened the floor for the audience to participate. People from the audience called out other names of Ancestors like Frederick Douglass, Sengbe Pieh, Ptahotep, Booker T. Washington, Marcus Garvey, Mary McCleoud Bethune, Malcolm X, Martin Luther King, Harriet Tubman, Nat Turner, Queen Hatshepsut,

Kwame Nkrumah, and Shaka Zulu. Some members of the audience spoke the names of deceased mothers, father, aunts, uncles, grandmothers, and grandfathers. Each time a name was spoken, Bro. Kofi would pour a few drops of water into the plant and everyone would say in a strong, unified voice, "ashe."

Finally, Bro. Kofi concluded by saying, "for all those named and unnamed we all say together…"

"Ashe!"

Moving the program along, Bro. Kofi summoned the Twelve Initiates to stand before him facing the audience. Then he said, "Brothers and sisters, these young men are here today as the final part of their rites of passage. They will be sharing some of the principles they have learned on their journey to manhood.

Daniel grew slightly nervous. In just a moment, all the Initiates would have to recite their Brotherhood Principles. These were the values that each of them swore to live by. Each principle spoke about being drug free, being committed to uplifting African people and humanity, pursuing education and knowledge of self, always respecting sisters and elders, and themselves, and developing their relationship with

God. After reciting these as a group, each brother had to recite a poem by himself.

When it was his turn, he rose and walked tall, not slouching as the Elders had warned him about. He thought about how strong he felt when he walked that way. As he came to the microphone, the audience awaited anxiously. Each of the young men before him had presented their poems impeccably and he wanted to be sure that he did just as well. As he looked out into the audience, he saw his mother and grandmother beaming with a look of pride. "My baby is growing into a man," his mother had said to him as they were about to leave the house for the community center that evening. He then saw Johnny and Jerome sitting in the back. They looked anxiously to see what he was going to say.

"Good evening, mothers, fathers, sisters, and brothers, he began. "I will be reciting Haki Madhubuti's poem 'The Book of Life.'"

Daniel began to think back to when Bro. Kofi first gave him that poem to memorize. He read through it, but didn't like it. "It doesn't even rhyme," he thought to himself. But as he took the time to memorize it and commit it not only to memory, but to *heart*, the poem began to have profound meaning to him. It was this profound meaning that he intended to dramatize as he presented the poem to the audience.

"You will recognize your brothers by the way they act and move throughout the world..." he began. In the audience, people's eyes got wide with attention and respect as he summoned his best speaking voice.

"There will be a strange force about them, there will be unspoken answers in them," he continued. Slowly his nervousness began to subside and with each verse of the poem he became more comfortable.

"This will be obvious not only to you, but to many. The confidence they have in themselves and in their people will be evident in their quiet saneness."

People in the audience started to look at each other in amazement at Daniel's oratorical skills.

"The way they relate to women will be clean, complimentary, responsible, and with honesty."

"That's right!" said an enthusiastic woman in the audience.

"The way they relate to children will be strong and soft, full of positive direction."

"Go'head brotha!" said another.

Daniel was basking in the responses and positive energy he was feeling from the audience. He continued as the amazement grew. The body of the poem talked about what people could expect from the faithful brothers who would step forward to lead African people.

"You will recognize these brothers..." Daniel concluded. Then with a penetrating gaze, he finished the last line, "...and they will not betray you."

The audience leapt to its feet shouting and applauding. The drummers played a loud and forceful drum roll. Daniel saw Johnny and Jerome. They were cheering and pumping their fists. He saw his mother. She looked so proud of her "baby boy." His grandmother wasn't clapping, however, she just stood awestruck with both hands over her mouth. It was as if she was looking at something different. Daniel, for a brief moment wondered what it was his grandmother was seeing. But then his attention returned to the overwhelming applause even as he took his seat.

The crowd's response reminded Daniel of how timid he had been when he first started the rites. He never wanted to stand in front of people and speak. But Bro. Kofi had coached him and encouraged him. "You have a gift, young brother. A gift is no good if it not given. You must share this gift with your people." Through the trials of the training, Daniel had overcome much of his shyness.

As he walked back to his seat, the drummer did another drum roll. When Daniel looked over at the drummers, he was amazed to see, that the man leading the drum roll was the same man he had seen in the park playing the drum. He looked at Daniel with a half-smile, then nodded to him. Daniel nodded back and took his seat.

As the ceremony concluded, all the Initiates were instructed to line up next to each other. Behind them, the Elders lined up.

"And now the final presentation," said Bro. Kofi. "These young men have demonstrated their commitment to their own self-development and the resurrection of African people and Humanity. To recognize their hard work, commitment, discipline, and completion of the rites of passage we will present each Initiate with a talisman. A talisman is an object which serves as a reminder of an important event in one's life. It usually takes the form of something worn around the neck. As such, the talisman that these young men will be presented with has on its leather cover the symbol *gye gyame*." Bro. Kofi held up the talisman for the audience to see. Then he held it up for the Initiates to see. It was beautiful. The brown leather cover was carefully stitched on the sides and the *gye gyame* was embroidered in the center in black.

"This symbol means, 'The Supreme God,'" Bro. Kofi continued. "This shows that you understand that African people always have and always must commit themselves to God. By accepting this, you are committing yourself to live not by the wicked ways of the world, but by the principles of your people."

Daniel was looking forward to wearing his talisman. He was very proud of how much he had grown over the course of the past nine months.

"Inside of the talisman," said Bro. Kofi, "is soil from Africa, the Motherland. It is taken from the Goree Island slave forts off the coast of Ghana and Senegal. This is the last African soil our Ancestors stood on before they were taken captive and brought here to America and enslaved. Wearing this talisman also symbolizes that you promise to one day go back to the homeland of your Ancestors. It is said that when one goes back to Africa, it is such a powerful experience, he will never be the same again. When you go, you must replace the soil in the talisman."

Bro. Kofi then called up each of the Initiates one by one as another of the Elders placed a talisman around their necks. The Intiates were then presented to the audience and the audience gave them each a round of applause. The drummers played a selection while the initiates went into the audience to stand with their families.

When Daniel stepped off of the stage, he tried to make his way through the crowd. Many people were patting him on the back and congratulating him. For some reason, he expected to see the old drummer man. He looked over at the drummers who were still keeping the rhythm of the ceremony going. The old man was no longer with the drummers. Daniel's mother made her way through the crowd and greeted him with a big hug. "Daniel, I'm so proud of you," she said as the tears rolled down her face. Then his grandmother hugged him and said, "Son, God is going to use you in a mighty way. She paused as if she was wondering whether she should say the next thing she was thinking. "Your father would have been so proud."

Daniel smiled, but felt a mixture of emotions. At first, he had a warm feeling inside from the love his mother and grandmother shared with him. But then he had a pain in his heart also because of the last words his grandmother said. "Your father would have been so proud," echoed in his head. The mixture of emotions from high to low and happy to sad clouded Daniel's mind. He wanted to cry. For it was nine years ago, around this same time of the year, that his father had been killed.

III

$\mathcal{D}$aniel slowly opened the front door. He was very careful to be quiet because it was at about this time that Grandma had a habit of dozing off to sleep in her rocking chair. Sure enough, when he got in the door and looked over into the living room, there she was – eyes closed with a thin blanket over her.

As he was about to put his first foot on the step to go upstairs and get washed up, he heard Grandma's chair rocking slowly.

"Boy, where you been?"

"Grandma?" said Daniel peering around the corner back into the living room. "I thought you were asleep."

"Every closed eye ain't sleep, boy, and every open eye ain't woke. Now where you been?"

"Oh. I was hanging out with Johnny and Jerome at the park. Then we went to the gym to play ball. I'm back on time. It's just starting to get dark," he said. He was worried that he might be in trouble, but try as he might, he couldn't think of anything he had done wrong.

"You're right. You're back on time. Come

on in here and sit down."

The room was dimly lit. There sat Grandma in her rocking chair. On the little table next to the lamp lay her Bible open with her reading glasses on top of it.

"Where's Momma?" asked Daniel.

"You know she's working late this week. She'll be home in a couple of hours."

Now Daniel remembered. Early that morning she had told him to be sure he had the kitchen clean by the time she got home.

"Daniel," said Grandma. "There are some things I need to share with you."

Daniel's stomach sank. Something within revealed to him that this was about his father's death. For years he had asked his mother and grandmother to tell him the whole story. Now that Grandma was ready to tell, he wasn't quite so sure he was ready.

"I need to share some things with you about your father," she said. I think that now you're ready."

Daniel nodded. His heart beat began to quicken.

"What I'm going to share with you are things I couldn't share with you when you were a young boy. But I can share it with you now that you are a young man."

Daniel's thoughts took him back to that

fateful day when Grandma picked him up from pre-school. She tried as best she could to explain to him what had happened to his Daddy. At four years old, however, Daniel didn't quite understand. He just kept asking her, "when is Daddy coming home?" The pain began to set in when his father never returned.

Now Daniel, though more mature, was still just as distraught over the untimely death of his father. He had trouble with the lump in his throat as he swallowed and took a deep breath.

Grandma looked away, off in the distance as if looking into the past. "Your father was so proud and happy when he found out your mother was pregnant. You see, I had quite a time trying to raise him. He got to hanging out in the streets, even causing trouble late at night. He even tried to bring some cigarettes in my house one day. I put my broomstick in his face and he knew I meant to use it, too. He was testing the limits. I wasn't about to let him bring that mess from the streets into my house."

"Lord, have mercy. He kept me on my knees praying. He got involved with a gang. When one of his best friends got shot and killed, that woke him up good. It was just before this that he met your mother. Seem like he fell in love instantly. He knew she wouldn't date him if he was in a gang."

"At his friend's funeral, he came up and gave his life to the Lord. I praised the Lord like never before. He vowed that he would get out of the gang. He said he no longer wanted to be a part of the problem, but part of the solution. He went back and told his friends he was getting out and tried to get them to stop, too. They threatened to kill him. Then I had to pray even harder."

"After he graduated from high school, he joined the army and went overseas. While overseas, he studied a great deal. He was stationed in Okinawa, Japan where he studied the martial arts. After two years in the army, he married your mother. A year later, they returned from Japan and said they were expecting you. He was so excited."

"Upon returning home, he joined the police force and returned to the same streets he used to run on. He had grown into such a fine man. He was so committed to trying to help people and trying to make the streets safe. He used to always say, 'I've got to clean up the streets so my son will have a safe place to live.'"

"A couple of your Daddy's friends actually left the gang with him. Some stayed behind. When he became a police officer, he ended up having to lock up some of his old gang partners. Though many in the neighborhood appreciated his work, the word on the street was that he needed to be killed.

"It always troubled your father that he had to lock up so many of our people. Our communities had become infested with drugs in a matter of a few years and he knew that those drugs were being dumped into our community by forces *outside* of our community. While overseas, your father took a trip to Africa. While there he bought a drum from a tribal elder. When he got back he began taking drumming lessons from a man. I never met the man, but your father always talked about him and respected him highly."

"He would come home late after working his shift and go into the basement. You and your Momma would be asleep. His job was so stressful and the only way he knew how to handle it was to go in the basement and play his drum. He would meditate and pray while playing and release the tension and the strain.

Daniel was spellbound as Grandma told the story. But at this point in the story, all the memories that he had kept inside came rushing back to him. He remembered, even as an infant and toddler hearing the booming bass from the drum as it rumbled through the floorboards of their house. He had come to enjoy it, and the rythms even lulled him to sleep some nights. It was a comforting sound that made him feel secure. He knew when he heard it that 'Daddy' was home and it created within him the same warm feeling he felt when his mother and grandmother hugged him at the ceremony.

"One day," Grandma continued, "some of the gang members were trying to rob a convenience store. When your father got to the scene, there was a heavy shootout. They had taken a little boy hostage."

At this point, Grandma's voice began to quiver. She was still trying to heal from the death of her only son.

They shot him three times in the chest. He was able to hang on for seven hours..."

Grandma couldn't continue. She and Daniel were both in tears. He went over to comfort her and then he saw it. There it was, behind the rocking chair.

"I've been saving this for nine years now, son. Your Daddy knew he wasn't going to make it. He told me that he saw the death angel coming for him. He told me to give this drum to you when you came of age. I had it re-skinned and touched up." She got up from the chair, picked up the large drum and handed it to Daniel.

His eyes were wide though still stained

with tears. He held the drum in his hands. He set it down and ran his hands across the goat skin that had been so carefully stretched over the top. Then he ran his hands over the mahogony. He began to take in the feel of the drum. Then he noticed that the *gye gyame*, the same symbol which was on his talisman, was carefully and creatively carved into the drum.

"Daniel," Grandma continued. "Last night I had a dream. I was walking through the park and I saw a man. He was dressed in African clothes and he was playing a drum just like this one. He began to talk to me like he knew me. He told me it was time for me to give the drum to you. He told me to send you to him and he would teach you."

Daniel didn't know what to think. He hadn't told Grandma about the man *he* had seen in the park and at the rites of passage ceremony.

"I been praying and fasting since you left this morning for school. I been reading my Bible trying to figure out what all this means. The Lord told me to just trust."

Then she reached in her purse, pulled out a crinkled $20 bill. "Tomorrow after school, you go to Heritage Park with your drum."

She pressed the money into his hand. "You give the man this money and take him the bag of fruit and vegetables I left in the refrigerator. Introduce yourself. Listen to what he tells you. Listen good. There's something special about this man. There's something special about this drum...and Daniel, there's something special about you."

IV

$\mathcal{D}$aniel entered the gates of Heritage Park with an eagerness in his walk. Though the big black duffel bag on his shoulder was heavy, right now he wasn't feeling the weight. He had carefully wrapped the drum in a towel and placed it in the bag. In one hand he had the bag of fruits and vegetables that Grandma had told him to give to the old man. His other hand was in his pocket feeling the crisp $20 bill he was to give the old man, too.

He had been anxious all day to go and meet the man for his first lesson. But how would he know if the man was going to be there. Again, the words of Grandma echoed in his mind, "The Lord told me to just trust."

As he passed through the gates and walked briskly past the pond, he heard something faint off in the distance. It was the drum! It sounded like the rhythm that had entranced him when he left Johnny and Jerome and chose to walk a different path. His choice to walk the different path led him to new horizons.

As he walked the path, he looked across the pond to where he heard the rhythm of the drum. But then his heart sank with disappointment. What he thought was the drum of the old man was actually a radio strapped to the back of a bike. The man riding the bike was bobbing his head up and down to the beat as he road through the park. The man wore a white tank top and shorts. His locked hair bounced with the beat. He road off along the path he was on, which led into a wooded area. The sound of the drums slowly faded away — away with Daniel's hopes of seeing the man that could teach him to walk in the steps of his father.

He walked on, head down, in disappointment. All of a sudden, the weight of the duffel bag became apparent. As he rounded the bend of the pond, he let out a deep sigh, more from his heart and soul than from his lungs. Then, again, off in the distance, he heard a beat and a rhythm.

Rounding the corner, he looked as far in the distance as he could and – there he was. It was the drummer. There he sat, as before, under the oak tree. As Daniel drew nearer, the sound grew louder and more pronounced.

Suddenly, the closer he came to the old man, the more apprehensive he became. What should he say to the man? "Um, excuse me sir... my grandmother had a dream about you and you're supposed to teach me how to play

the drum?!" He didn't know this man. How
could he just walk up to him?

There was something within pulling on
Daniel that would not let him walk away. There
was something wrapped up in the destiny of
the moment which made Daniel summon a bold-
ness above and beyond himself.

The old man's eyes were closed in a medi-
tative mood as he continued drumming. He sat
on a folding chair. There was also another folding chair leaning against the tree. The drum sat
between his knees. His hands were cupped and
sometimes flat as he beat different parts of the
drum – sometimes the center of the drum, sometimes along the outer edges. Daniel noticed
that the closer he hit the drum to the center,
the deeper the tone. The closer the man hit to
the edges, the higher the pitch.

Now Daniel, about ten yards away, wondered, "what am I going to say to this man? I
can't turn back." Just then, the man opened his
eyes and looked at Daniel. It was as if he knew
Daniel were approaching the whole time.

"So you received my message, young
brother?" said the old man with half a smile.

"Message?" Daniel replied.

"Yes...the message."

Daniel looked confused. He still didn't
know what to say.

"Why did you come here?" said the old man.

Daniel took the drum from the duffel bag and set it down on the grass.

"I like the way you play the drum. I was wondering if you could teach me."

"That's a good lookin' drum you got there, brother. Where'd you get it from?"

"It was my Dad's," said Daniel proudly.

The old man got up and looked the drum over. He ran his hands along the mahogany stem and the goat skin top. Then he looked back at Daniel.

"Peace and blessings, young brother. My name is Bro. Babatunde."

Daniel shook his hand. Bro. Babatunde's grip was tight. Daniel remembered that the Elders taught him in the rites of passage to shake a person's hand firmly and look them in the eye.

"My name is Daniel."

"Brother Daniel, I would be honored to teach you the ancient African art of drumming. However, it is not easy and it takes great discipline and commitment."

"I will do my best," said Daniel eagerly.

"Have a seat," said Bro. Babatunde, opening the folding chair leaning against the tree. Daniel felt a sense of relief. He had mustered the courage to follow his intuition and approach the man. So far, things were working out well.

"What does your name mean?" asked Daniel.

"Babatunde means, 'father' or 'elder returns'," said Bro. Babatunde.

"Where are you from?" asked Daniel.

"I come from Ghana. It is on the west coast of Africa."

Daniel didn't quite understand the meaning of Bro. Babatunde's name, but he was very anxious to get started with his drumming lessons.

You look like you're ready to begin," said Bro. Babatunde.

Daniel nodded his head eagerly.

"What do you know about drumming, Bro. Daniel?"

"Not much," said Daniel. "I mean…I just like the way it sounds and the way it makes me feel."

"Do you know what kind of drum that you have there?"

"No."

"This is called a *djembe drum*," said Bro. Babatunde. "It is native to many west African nations. It is a very powerful instrument."

"I could hear you drumming all the way on the other side of the park," said Daniel.

Yes…" said Bro. Babatunde, "…and I was only playing lightly," he said with a laugh.

"Lightly?"

"You see, brother, the djembe can actually be heard up to 20 miles away when played a certain way. Other drums, like the talking drum can be heard up to five miles away."

"This little thing can be heard 20 miles away? How?" asked Daniel.

"Look over there," said Bro. Babatunde. He pointed off in the distance to a man walking on the paved path through the park. Do you see the brother on the cell phone over there?"

"Yes," replied Daniel.

"He is holding a modern communication device in his hand. You call it a telephone and it can be used to talk to people many miles away. What you are holding in you hands is an ancient communication device. It can be used to send and receive messages. Both use the technology of sound waves."

"How were they able to make the drum so that it could send messages so far?" asked Daniel.

"This drum brings together all the elements of the circle of life."

"Huh?" said Daniel.

"To activate this drum, this ancient African communication device, four things are needed: wood from a tree, the skin of a goat, human hands, and the spirit of God moving through the body of the drummer. With these, you can communicate with people further away than you think."

"I didn't know people had that kind of knowledge in Africa...and so many years ago."

"Young brother, the knowledge, wisdom, and insights that we had then far exceeds what we have today in this so-called modern age of technology."

"What do you mean? They didn't have computers, phones, satellites, and space shuttles."

"But they did have loving communities in which families were together. They didn't have to worry about crime and violence. They didn't have to worry about children being disrespectful or dropping out of school. They were in touch with the spirit much unlike society today. To be in touch with the spirit is the highest technology possible. It will allow you to send and receive messages that others cannot. This is why we must reconnect to our roots."

"Man...I never thought of it that way," said Daniel.

"Soon, as a result of studying the drum, you will think like this more often," said Bro. Babatunde.

"So the drum wasn't just used to play

music then?" asked Daniel.

"Oh no, Brother. It was used for much more than that. It was used to communicate with and welcome the Most High and the presence of the Ancestors. It was used for meditation, prayer, and healing. It was used in the everyday life of the people in all tribes. African ceremonies, rituals, and festivals always included the drum. It was considered a sacred object. If a drummer practices his art correctly, he will never be sick, tense, or stressed. All of this is released through the playing of the drum."

"I didn't know playing the drum was that deep," said Daniel. I thought anyone could do it. I thought it was just about putting together a rhythm."

"Most people think as you did. It is only due to a lack of knowledge. During the times of slavery, the white man knew that the drum of the African had power, but he didn't understand it. He knew that somehow we were communicating, planning revolts, calling for help, transmitting news from plantation to plantation using the drum. So he outlawed all drums. When our white brothers came into Africa, seeking to rule and ruin, they acted as if the drum were demonic and satanic. They said we were calling upon evil spirits. They did not understand us and didn't seek to understand us. They destroyed our drums—thousands of them, along with our way of life."

Daniel was deeply drawn into Bro. Babatunde's words. He didn't realize that a history lesson came along with the drumming lessons, but he was taking it all in. He asked questions to gain greater insight into the knowledge and wisdom Bro. Babatunde was sharing. The sun was setting over the trees behind the Heritage Park pond. The sky was orange, rust, and golden. Finally, after about sixty minutes, Bro. Babatunde brought their discussion to a close.

"Well, that's all for today."

"But what about the drumming. I mean…you didn't show me how to hit the drum or play any rhythms or anything."

"In due time, young brother. In due time," said Bro. Babatunde patiently.

"How long have you been drumming?" asked Daniel.

"Hah!" said Bro. Babatunde laughing. "I have been drumming longer than you and your mother have been alive…combined."

"How long will it take for me to get as good as you."

"It will take time, young brother. But don't just focus on the destination of being a master drummer. Enjoy the journey."

"Well is there anything I can practice while I'm at home until our next meeting."

"As a matter of fact, yes," said Bro. Babatunde.

Daniel began to get excited. Maybe he would learn and practice a special technique.

"Set your drum aside," said Bro. Babatunde. "Now sit up straight in your chair. Close your eyes."

Daniel obeyed dutifully. Still in the back of his mind, he wondered what this had to do with drumming.

"Now…I want you to put your right hand on your stomach. Breathe in deeply, then breathe out."

Daniel breathed in and puffed his chest out, then exhaled.

"You made the same mistake that most people do," said Bro. Babatunde. "This time, when you breathe in, let your stomach come out. When you exhale, your stomach should come in."

Daniel tried it. It felt awkward at first.

"This is proper breathing. It is called abdominal breathing. Now close your eyes. Inhale…exhale…inhale….exhale.

Daniel felt his mind body, and spirit begin to relax. It was as though his body was weightless.

"Feel yourself getting lighter. Now take your mind back to all the things we have talked about. Turn these things over in your mind...the history of the drum...the technology of the drum...the sacredness of the drum. Give thanks for all the blessings bestowed upon you by the Creator...inhale...exhale. Now open your eyes.

Daniel opened his eyes. He felt refreshed and rejuvenated.

"Practice this for at least five minutes when you wake up every morning and before you go to sleep. It will increase your endurance and allow you to express yourself with great precision and proficiency on the drum."

Okay," said Daniel.

"I will see you on Wednesday and we will continue."

Daniel got up and packed his drum inside his bag.

"Oh yeah," he said, digging in his pocket. "My grandmother told me to give you this." He handed the folded $20 bill to Bro. Babatunde. Then he reached into the bag and pulled out a small bag of fruits and vegetables. He handed those also to Bro. Babatunde.

"Thank you for teaching me." He held out his hand to Bro. Babatunde.

"Thank you. It is an honor and a privilege," said Bro. Babatunde extending his hand also. "Please give your grandmother and your mother my regards." As they shook hands, Bro. Babatunde looked him deep in the eyes.

"You have a good spirit, young Daniel. You will do many great and wonderful things for your people and for Humanity. I will see you Wednesday."

Daniel smiled. He threw his duffel bag over his shoulder and headed off on the path which led out of the park.

V

When Daniel got home that evening, he found his grandmother sitting in the living room in her rocking chair. Again, she looked like she was asleep. He wasn't sure whether to speak or not. If she was asleep, he didn't want to wake her. But then, he didn't want to assume, as he had done before, that she was asleep.

"Grandma?!" he said nudging her lightly. "Are you awake?"

"I am now," she said slowly opening her eyes and yawning. "I was out in the garden for four hours today. I guess I wore myself out. Well…tell me about your drumming lesson. Was the man there in the park?

"Yes." replied Daniel.

His grandmother's old eyes lit up with excitement.

"He was just like you described him." Daniel went on to share all that he had learned, sparing no details. "…but I didn't get a chance to actually do any drumming," he concluded.

"In due time, Daniel. In due time," she said smiling.

"That's exactly what he said."

"Well...he's obviously preparing you for something wonderful. Did you give him the money and the bag of fruit and vegetables?"

"Yes, ma'am. He said 'thank you.'"

"It's just like the vision I had," said Grandma, obviously pleased. "Praise the Lord."

"Can I go upstairs and practice my breathing now?"

"Yes, but go get some dinner first...it's on the stove. Put all the food up. Then make sure your room is straight, your mother will be home in a little while."

"Okay."

Daniel woke up Wednesday morning, anxious as ever to have his second lesson. He was careful to be sure to do his breathing exercises. He rushed off to school finding it difficult to concentrate in his classes. After school, he went home to check on his grandmother. After a small snack, he put his drum into the large duffel bag and set off for Heritage Park.

The sun was shining bright, another beautiful day. The ducks quacked as he walked hurriedly by the pond. The landscape was a vibrant and lush green. The workers from the city must have been by early that morning to cut the grass.

The lines from the mowers were still visible in the grass. Daniel took it all in as he made his way around the pond. Then the familiar sounds of the Motherland filled the air as Bro. Babatunde's drum called out to him. He smiled and quickened his step.

"Peace be unto you, young Daniel," greeted Bro. Babatunde. It was if he was as eager to see Daniel as Daniel was to see him.

"Peace, Bro. Babatunde," said Daniel with a smile.

"Come...sit," he said, motioning for Daniel to sit on the folding chair he had just set out.

Daniel sat down and pulled his drum from the duffel bag.

"I'll actually get to drum today, right?" asked Daniel anxiously.

"Yes. But first we must see how well your breathing is and we must prepare the body to endure the drumming."

"Oh, yeah...I practiced just like you said."

"Okay. Set your drum to the side. Sit up straight. Close your eyes. Right hand on your stomach. Inhale, let your stomach come out. Exhale, let your stomach come in. Inhale...exhale."

Daniel, following Bro. Babatunde's directives, felt himself feeling more in tune. He could feel an energy pulsing through his body. It started from his stomach and ran throughout his body.

"See yourself," said Bro. Babatunde. "See yourself playing the drum with confidence and precision. See yourself calling others to the drum, just as you have been called here to learn. Inhale. Exhale. Three more times. Inhale. Exhale...now open your eyes."

Again, Daniel felt refreshed and ready.

"Now we must stretch. Do as I do."

Bro. Babatunde lifted his arms in front of himself to eye level. He kept his wrists loose so that his hands looked suspended in air. He slowly began to move his arms up and down in a fluid and poetic motion. Moving his arms up, he inhaled. Moving his arms down, he exhaled. Daniel did his best to keep up. In the back of his mind, he was still wondering why they were not yet playing the drum. Then the words of his grandmother echoed in his head, "Listen to what he tells you. Listen good. There's something special about this man."

After about a minute of the stretches, Bro. Babatunde then moved each arm outward in a circular motion. Again, Marcus followed as best he could.

"Don't slouch...sit up straight, Bro. Daniel," said Bro. Babatunde.

Daniel's inquisitiveness got the best of him and he asked, "Why are we doing this?"

"We are activating the life force energy within. We are opening the channels and gateways for the energy to travel so that we can put that energy into the drum and transform it into vibration. Does that answer your question?"

Daniel just smiled and shook his head "no."

"I didn't think it would, but soon you'll understand. They continued with a number of stretches for about ten minutes. Then Bro. Babatunde told Daniel to pick up his drum.

"In the sitting position, with your back straight, pull your feet together, but keep your knees apart. Place the drum between your knees,"" he said demonstrating. "Press your knees together to hold the drum in place.

Daniel did as he was instructed as Bro. Babatunde demonstrated once more. He was following well, but it was not easy.

"I didn't know playing the drum was so technical," said Daniel as he moved the drum in place between his knees.

"Most people don't," said Bro. Babatunde. "Keep your feet together and stay on your toes. This is why breathing is so important. You must have the proper endurance to be a drummer. Most African rituals and ceremonies last at least two hours."

"Two hours?!" said Daniel.

"Yes, just like your rites of passage ceremony. So if this appears difficult, consider the fact that you haven't even started drumming yet."

Daniel struggled to get his drum in proper position and his feet properly placed.

"Okay, you're all set now. Now hold it in place."

Bro. Babatunde then began to explain how the drum was put together and what it could do.

"The goatskin that covers this drum was chosen for a couple of reasons: it's strong and tough, but also pliable and flexible."

Daniel looked intently at Bro. Babatunde, taking in everything he said. He slowly ran his hands across the goat skin.

"Now, there are six basic tones on the djembe. The first one is the *bass*." He hit the center of the drum with his cupped hand.

"BOOM," sounded the drum.

"The second one is *song*,"

BA DAA," sounded the drum as he hit it.

"The third one is *solo*."

"BING!"

The fourth one is *variation*."

BE DEE!"

The fifth one is *ka*."

BAP!"

"And the sixth one is called *press ka.*"
BOM!"

"Now try each one after me. When you hit the middle of the drum you will cup your hands. The closer you get to the edge, you will use the tips of your fingers."

Daniel imitated each tone that Bro. Babatunde played.

"Very good. You are progressing nicely.

Bro. Babatunde continued drilling Daniel until the sun began to set. The sky was no longer bright and golden, but crimson, rust, and orange. Daniel was sweating profusely and breathing at a rate faster than normal. The joints in his legs and back ached from being locked for the past 90 minutes. His hands were throbbing from pounding the drum so much.

"That will be all for today," said Bro. Babatunde. "Practice your breathing exercises and the six tones. Watch your posture carefully. Before you go, let's practice the breathing one more time."

As Daniel practiced his breathing, his heart rate slowed down and he began to feel more relaxed. His body felt light. His mind felt lighter.

When they finished with the breathing exercise, Daniel packed up his drum, gave Bro.

Babatunde a bag of apples, oranges, and bananas, and headed toward Independence Avenue, back home.

"Brother Daniel," called Bro. Babatunde. Daniel turned around.

"When you get home, soak your hands in salt water for an hour before going to bed."

Without really understanding, Daniel simply replied "Okay" and kept on walking.

He felt good. He finally got to learn some of the techniques and play the drum. The sky was mesmerizing as the sun set over the trees behind the pond at Heritage Park. And while that sun was setting over the trees behind the pond, Daniel felt as though a sun, just as bright and vibrant, was rising in his life.

VI

$\mathcal{D}$aniel sat on the side of his bed thinking about how much he had learned about the djembe. For the past three months, Bro. Babatunde had been instructing him in the ancient art of drumming. Each day they practiced the six tones, basic rhythms, proper breathing and posture, and the spiritual essence behind the craft. Bro. Babatunde carefully wove history and culture into each lesson to let him know about the ceremonies and rituals in which the drum was used. Three times a week he would sit at the feet of the master, giving fruits, vegetables, and $20 in return.

Bro. Babatunde didn't seem to mind teaching him for so little. Each practice session would last usually from two and a half to three hours. He had shown great patience and skill in training Daniel. Daniel appreciated how Bro. Babatunde was able to bring forth abilities that he didn't even know he had. He would always practice diligently on the nights he didn't have instruction.

Once when he hadn't practiced, Bro. Babatunde noticed. "Bro. Daniel, when you don't practice, you are only holding back your own development. You are not fooling me." Daniel knew he was right. When he neglected to soak his hands after practice, the joints in his hands throbbed and ached with pain. He had learned the hard way to follow all of Bro. Babatunde's directives closely and completely.

Now that it was summertime, Daniel didn't have to worry about rushing home to finish his homework. He could put the majority of his energies into practicing.

He picked up his drum and walked downstairs. He peeked in the living room where his grandmother was watching the evening news.

"Grandma, I'm going downstairs to practice. Do you need anything before I go?"

"No sweetheart. Go on ahead."

He walked down the basement stairs lugging the drum under his arm.

He turned on the old lamp and took a seat in the dimly lit room. Grandma had told him that the old folding chair he was now using, was the same one his father used. He looked around the room. In the corner was an old black and white TV with a hanger stuck in the left antenna. The TV was rarely used. Everything in the basement seemed to be a permanent monument to the past.

The truth was, everything was the same since Daniel's father had passed. He had started trying to remodel the basement room, but he had only just begun when his life ended. So, just about everything was as he left it. Daniel's mother was working too much to even think about doing anything with the basement. It just wasn't a priority. Grandma spent most of her time in her garden, the kitchen, and the living room. So Daniel claimed the basement as his own.

The old black and white TV was sitting on top of a tattered green army trunk. It had a rusty combination lock on it. Daniel had never taken much notice of it before. Why he noticed it today, he didn't know. He sat up straight to begin his meditation and breathing exercises. He took several deep breaths and exhales. It focused him. After about five minutes he was ready to continue his preparation.

He then stretched for another five minutes, being sure to use precision. When he finished stretching, he began to position himself to play his drum. With the drum between his knees, he began playing the six tones followed by a basic rhythm. Bro. Babatunde had taught him to play meditatively – that is, playing a repetitive beat while using proper breathing. The repetition along with the beat always took

Daniel to a place of peace in his own mind and spirit.

As he beat the drum, his mind began to clear even more. "Ahhh," whispered Daniel to himself. He no longer had to think about breathing properly, now it just came naturally. He felt gateways and pathways of energy within being opened as he channeled the flow of his internal energy into the drum.

Then something unusual began to happen. Though his eyes were closed, he began to see lights flickering. These were not lights in the room, but in his mind's eye. He felt a strong presence of energy pulling on him. The rhythm of the beat seemed to intensify, but not with his permission or consent. It was as if he was no longer playing. It was really as if something else, was expressing itself and playing *through* him. This unusual presence and energy pulled on him more, but he resisted. Instinctively, he knew this thing was stronger than him. Where did this thing want to take him?

The lights stopped flickering and came together in the form of the sun, shining bright. Beneath the sun it looked like a group of people standing in a circle. It was all so blurry. He couldn't make out any features.

Fear, quickly prevailed over Daniel's curiosity. Whatever this was, it was seeking to take him into the unknown. He wasn't ready to go. He had never had an experience like this before. His hands seemed now to have a mind of their own and had picked up the pace of the beat. He focused all of his energy in his hands and willed them to stop playing. They would not. He tried even harder, harnessing his will. Finally, his hands stopped.

He opened his eyes. He was sweating…dripping as if he had just stepped out of the rain. He wiped his brow, then looked at his hands. They were trembling. He still felt a sense of fear. It made him want to run upstairs and leave the drum in the basement. Then his attention was turned to the old army trunk that the TV was sitting on.

He set the drum aside and went over to the trunk. He lifted the TV and moved it to the floor. He put his hands on the rusted combination lock. He gently pulled it and it popped open.

The trunk creaked as he opened it slowly. It smelled like it had been shut for several years. Inside were clothes. Whose clothes they were he didn't know. Normally, he would have lost interest but something moved him to continue looking. It was the same presence he experienced while he was drumming. He wiped away the sweat that had crept upon his forehead again and picked up the first item of clothing. It, like the trunk, was army green. It was an army uniform. Then, of course, Daniel knew whose it was. It was his father's.

Underneath the army uniform was a picture of his father in his uniform. Also there was an old picture of Daniel's father and mother. His mother appeared to be pregnant.

Daniel searched through the trunk some more. Underneath the army uniform and pictures was something blue – navy blue. As Daniel unfolded it, he noticed that it was another uniform. It was a police uniform. As he held it up and it unfolded completely, and something fell out. It startled Daniel and he jumped back. Then, looking on the floor, he noticed that it was his father's badge. He looked over it carefully. It was shiny and silver. It had numbers along the bottom.

Daniel felt strange looking through the remaining items of his father. At first, he felt sad. Then he felt happy as he reminisced about good times like going to the carnival and the movies. He remembered his father tossing a football with him in the back yard when he was four. He taught him how to catch. They used to go out every night after dinner and practice. It took him two weeks to learn how to catch that little football and his dad was so proud when he did.

Just then, he looked down, past the uniform and noticed another picture. It was his father in the police uniform. Under that was a picture of him with his father. Daniel had a small football in his hand.

The joy of reminiscing about these good times quickly faded and became more than Daniel could bear. He wanted to cry, but wouldn't let himself. He quickly threw the clothes and pictures back into the trunk and ran upstairs. He ran all the way up to his room and sat on the edge of his bed. "Why did he have to die? Why did he leave us?" he thought uncontrollably. Daniel knew that if he was going to have any peace of mind, that these questions needed answers.

VII

Daniel walked down Independence Avenue toward the Heritage Park Community Center. As he walked, he looked into the windows of all the stores, shops, and boutiques. He passed Black to Basics Bookstore. He thought back to his rites of passage and how each of the Twelve Initiates had to go there and purchase the books they had to read for the training.

Then there was Jackson's General Store on the corner of Independence and Liberation. The Elders had negotiated a price with Mr. Jackson, so that the Twelve Intiates could purchase their camping supplies there. The Elders made sure that everything that was needed for the manhood training was purchased in the community. This taught the Initiates to do the same. Daniel waved to Mr. Jackson through the window.

Just down from Jackson's General Store was Nia's African Fashions where the Initiates had to purchase their outfits for the rites of passage ceremony. Daniel had been worried when the Elders told them that they would need $100 to participate in the rites. But the Elders showed each of the Intiates how to raise the money together. None of the parents of the Initiates had to pay. The boys arranged with Mr. Jackson to sell vegetables from their garden at the general store. They had car washes in the community. They went to several of the churches in the community and offered their services to clean sanctuaries, fellowship halls, and parking lots. The Elders saw to it that the boys did an outstanding job every time. They were not allowed to leave a work site until their work had met the specifications of the Elders.

As Daniel continued down Independence Avenue, finally, the community center was in sight. Standing out front were Johnny and Jerome. Jerome was talking to Johnny. His hands were flapping in the air. Jerome was yelling and very clearly upset. Daniel wondered what had happened to get Jerome in such a frenzy.

"I thought y'all were gonna be inside playing ball," said Daniel as he walked up to them.

"Man that nigga is trippin'!" yelled Jerome pointing inside the community center. "Forget him!"

"What happened?" said Daniel to Johnny.

Jerome was now walking in circles enraged. He looked as if he were about to explode at any minute.

"We were playing ball and Jerome kept cursing on the court and playing too rough. Mr. Smith told him to settle down or he would have to leave. He kept it up and started arguing with Mr. Smith and they put him out."

"Man you know they got that rule that you can't curse in or around the community center," said Daniel.

"Nigga you must be trippin', too. Man we were just playing ball. So what if we curse sometimes. That's what people do when they play ball. Then he gonna start pointin' at me and tell me to leave. I got somethin' for him though," said Jerome.

Bits and pieces of lessons began to run through Daniel's mind. The Elders had taught the Intiates that a man only curses because he doesn't have the vocabulary to properly express himself. Once when one of the Initiates had slipped and used profanity, he had to stay in the push-up position for twenty minutes while reciting his principles. He couldn't rest. If he refused, he would be out of the manhood training.

On another occasion, Daniel had slipped and referred to one of the brothers as a "nigga." Bro. Kofi exploded. None of the brothers had ever seen him so upset before or since. He always had such a calm and peaceful spirit.

"You've been in this rites of passage for six months and you still haven't figured out that we're not niggas?!"

As a result, Daniel had to spend 30 minutes in the push-up position. He remembered how his arms felt like rubber when he finished. His arms felt like they were going to fall off. But he learned the lesson that he should not refer to his own people, or any people for that matter, by such a derogatory name.

"Yeah, that wasn't right for him to put Jerome out," said Johnny. Johnny didn't seem to share Jerome's rage. As a matter of fact, it seemed to Daniel that he was just going along with Jerome's anger. But Johnny knew Jerome was wrong – Daniel could tell.

"He's always making people do laps and puttin' people out!" continued Jerome.

"What do you mean?!" He puts people out if they break the rules," said Daniel trying to reason with him.

"Well he shouldn't have put me out. I got somethin' for him!"

"What do you mean you 'got somethin' for him?'"

Jerome pulled out a switchblade.

Johnny's eyes bulged. He looked as if he couldn't believe that Jerome was going to take it to that extreme.

"Man are you crazy?!" said Daniel. "You're gonna try to cut Mr. Smith?"

"Naw man! I ain't *that* crazy. But I am crazy enough to slit the tires on his new truck, cut up those nice leather seats and run my keys all over that beautiful paint job," he said with a devilish grin.

"Man, you don't want to do that. I'm telling you...he'll figure out it was you!"

"He ain't gonna know if nobody tells him!" retorted Jerome glaring at Daniel. "So c'mon, let's go." Jerome walked off around the corner to the parking lot behind the community center. Daniel looked at Johnny. Daniel knew they had to stop him.

As they made their way around the corner to the parking lot, Jerome was pacing back and forth. "Yeah, I'm gonna show him not to git in my face like that again," he was saying to himself. It was like Jerome was waiting for them to get there so he could show how big and bad he was. There behind him was a brand new, sparkling clean, black truck. Even the tires were shining. It appeared that Mr. Smith must have washed it that morning.

Daniel seemed to be overtaken by the spirit that Jerome had. The negative energy was so strong and overpowering. Daniel had to find out a way to keep Jerome from making a life-altering decision, and he knew he couldn't necessarily count on Johnny for help.

"Yo man...I can't let you do this," said Daniel walking toward Jerome. Jerome didn't seem the least bit convinced by Daniel's reason. He just took a step closer to the truck and bent down, ready to slit the tires.

Daniel lunged toward him and grabbed his arm. "DON'T DO IT, MAN!"

"Nigga, git your hands offa me!" yelled Jerome, pushing Daniel's hand away. Do I have to cut you first before I do this?! Now you're Mr. Africa since you been in manhood training and drumming and all that stuff!"

Now Daniel was really in trouble. The negative energy that Jerome had was first being directed at Mr. Smith. Now it was being directed at *him*. He had seen Jerome angry before. He had even seen him ready to fight. But Jerome had never turned on *him*. A part of him felt sad. A part of him was deeply concerned. A part of him also felt angry. "Well if he wants to fight, bring it on!" thought the angry side of Daniel in his mind. Then the concerned side spoke: "find a way to stall him."

So there they stood staring at each other, shoulders square, toe to toe. Johnny stood watching in disbelief. Jerome threw the knife on the ground.

"I don't even need a knife to take you out!"

Daniel stepped back and in his best trash-talking voice yelled, "C'mon, then!!!" He thought if he yelled loud enough, someone inside the community center would hear it, come outside, and break it up.

"Why are you backing up then? Come on!"

"Hey! What are you guys doing?!" yelled a security officer from the back door of the community center. He was tall and muscular with a deep voice. Jerome and Daniel both froze. As the officer walked closer, he began to recognize Jerome.

"Aren't you the one Coach Smith just put out?!" yelled the officer. Jerome just looked down in silence and embarrassment.

"I guess it wasn't enough that you got put out...now you wanna come back here and act a fool?! Well, come on. We'll call your parents...and if that doesn't work then we'll just go on down to juvenile lock up."

Jerome walked with his head down toward the officer. Daniel slowly put his foot over the knife that Jerome had thrown down and carefully slid it under the truck. He didn't want the officer to see that Jerome had a weapon, otherwise Jerome might end up locked up.

"Do you two need to have your parents called, too?" said the officer pointing at Daniel and Johnny.

"No," said Johnny holding up his hands.

"No sir," said Daniel.

"Then get outta here!"

Daniel and Johnny needed no other warnings. They walked quickly around the corner and went home.

VIII

Daniel sat on the side of his bed packing his duffel bag. He carefully placed a small blanket over and around his drum. After he wrapped it up, he placed it in the duffel bag and zipped it up. Throwing the bag on his shoulder, he skipped down the steps and went into the kitchen. His grandmother was busy at the stove making dinner. Daniel looked in the refrigerator and grabbed the bag of vegetables his grandmother had left for him to give to Bro. Babatunde.

"I'm going to drumming practice, Grandma," he said giving her a kiss on the cheek.

"Okay. Dinner will be ready when you get back so don't stop at the store buying junk food."

"Yes Ma'am."

As Daniel entered the gates of Heritage Park, his mind was mixed up with many emotions. He thought about the fight he and Jerome almost had. Then he thought about the experience he had playing the drum in the basement and finding his father's uniforms and pictures. All these thoughts swirled around in his mind.

Daniel was finding it increasingly difficult just to do something that everybody had to do in their lives – grow up. As he rounded the bend of the pond, he saw Bro. Babatunde sitting under the oak tree. But he wasn't playing his drum. He was sitting there eating something. Walking closer, he saw that Bro. Babatunde was eating a mango.

"Peace, Bro. Daniel," said Bro. Babatunde chewing the last bits of mango.

"Peace, Bro. Babatunde."

"Tell your grandmother that the mangoes she sent me from the Farmer's Market were the best!" he said with a smile. "Go ahead and do your stretches while I get ready…then do the rhythm of the harvest that we were working on during the last lesson." He then took out a water bottle and took a sip. Then he took out a handkerchief, wet it with the water from the water bottle, and wiped his hands and mouth.

Daniel sat down. Pulled out his carefully-wrapped drum from the duffel bag, then began his stretches. After stretching, Daniel began playing the rhythm of the harvest. His mind, however, was still not on the drumming. It was still jumbled with the events of the past two days. It was easy to see and hear, that he was not focused on his drumming.

"Bro. Daniel," said Bro. Babatunde with

a look of concern. "What are you doing?"

"I'm playing the rhythm of the harvest," said Daniel, not realizing how terrible he sounded.

"No you're not. I don't know what that is you were playing. But I *do* know you weren't focused and you weren't using proper technique. Even your breathing was off."

Daniel just put his head down.

"But I was playing it really well at home."

"Is something on your mind?"

Daniel took a deep breath and let out a sigh. Where should he begin.

He explained the story of his situation with Jerome. He explained why Jerome was put out of the community center and how he wanted to vandalize Mr. Smith's truck. It was still a mystery to Daniel why Jerome had turned on him. The two hadn't talked since the incident.

"Are these the two boys I saw you with on the day we met?" said Bro. Babatunde, following the whole story closely.

"Yes," said Daniel. "I mean...Jerome and Johnny are my best friends, but Jerome was just out of control yesterday. I can't hang out with him if he's just gonna snap like that and get us in trouble. But we've been friends a long time."

"Bro. Daniel," said Bro. Babatunde, "I'm very proud of you. You looked deep within to help keep your friend from making a terrible decision. You even found a way to keep from fighting. You are truly a mighty warrior."

This made Daniel feel better, but it still didn't solve the problem. "Well, what should I do now?"

"Go to your friend. Hopefully, now that he's had some time to cool down, you can talk with him reasonably. Perhaps he will listen and see the error of his ways."

"I don't know," said Daniel. "He was pretty upset."

"Take courage and be confident, young brother. He'll listen."

"Okay," said Daniel

"Is something else wrong?"

Daniel hesitated. He didn't know how to share his feelings about his father's death with Bro. Babatunde. He had told Bro. Babatunde some time ago that his father was deceased, but he didn't go into details. But certainly Bro. Babatunde would have some insight into what happened while Daniel was playing the drum and had the vision.

"Well...something happened the other night while I was playing the drum. I mean...I did my breathing exercises and stretches and then started practicing the rhythms we went over. It was like I didn't even have to think about my breathing or technique. It was all coming together perfectly. Everything was just flowing. It sounded a lot like when you play. Then, all of a sudden—"

"You saw lights, flickering lights," said Bro. Babatunde completing the thought for him. He looked off in the direction of the pond.

"Yeah!" said Daniel looking up at him in surprise. "How did you know?"

"You are progressing at a rapid rate, Bro. Daniel. Now you are tapping into the timeless secrets of the drummer. Tell me what else happened."

"I…I got scared. I started seeing a circle of people. I couldn't stop my hands. I kept trying to pull them away from the drum…it was like they had a mind of their own. I was scared…I 've never had …an out of body experience before."

"You were being called to the cypher," said Bro. Babatunde, still looking off thoughtfully in the distance. It was as if he were thinking of how to explain it to Daniel.

"The what?"

"The cypher. A cypher is a circle. You were being called to the cypher of the Ancestors."

Daniel just looked confused.

"Do you remember during some of the

first lessons when I told you that our people used the drums to communicate with God and the Ancestors. You are reaching that level and it is for a very powerful reason," said Bro. Babatunde.

"I'm afraid," said Daniel looking away, and obviously embarrassed about it.

"You must face your fears, Bro. Daniel. Fear is only *false evidence appearing real.* You have been summoned by the Ancestors"

"I don't think I'm ready for this."

"Just by virtue of the fact that the Ancestors have summoned you means that you are ready. But you must have courage."

Daniel still looked disillusioned.

"Bro. Daniel, do you know what an impala is?"

"Yeah…it's a big car. A Chevy, I think."

"Yes…" said Bro. Babatunde laughing. "It is a car, but it is also an animal. It is a type of antelope that lives in southern Africa and other parts of the Motherland. The African impala can jump to a height of over 10 feet and cover a distance greater than 30 feet. Yet zoo keepers can keep the impala locked up with a wall that's only three feet high."

"How can they do that if the impala can jump so high. Wouldn't it just jump over the wall and escape?" asked Daniel.

"Well, the impala will only jump if it can see where its feet will fall. If it can't see where it will fall, it won't jump. It is a matter of faith, Bro. Daniel. The impala could be free if only it had faith in where it would land. Bro. Daniel, *you* are the impala. The Ancestors have summoned you for a reason. Many are called, but few are *chosen*. *You* have been chosen, but you must have faith that you will be protected."

"How can I overcome my fear?"

There are several things you must do. I can help you, but I cannot do it for you. Are you willing to heed the call of the Ancestors?"

Daniel hesitated again. But something was pulling on him. It was subduing his fears long enough for him to make a clear decision.

"Yes," he said definitively. "I want to answer the call."

"Here is what you must do. Go home and seek to make amends with your friend. Meditate and pray before going to bed. Wake up at 6:00, before the sun rises. Wash your face, your eyes, inside your nose and ears. Then go into meditation and prayer again. Give thanks for your many blessings. Ask the Most High for guidance on your journey and the courage to complete it. Now tomorrow, you must not eat or drink anything except water. Help your grandmother around the house and do not watch television. All of this is for the purpose of cleansing your mind and spirit. I want you to come back to the park with your drum at 7:30 pm. Do you understand?"

"Yes," said Daniel taking a deep breath. By this time, over an hour had passed as they had discussed Daniel's dilemma.

"We will stop the lesson for this evening. I think we've done enough."

Bro. Babatunde turned around and reached inside a small bag that he always carried. Daniel could never really tell what was in it other that the fruit, vegetables, and bottle of water he often had. He pulled out something folded that was bright and white. As Bro. Babatunde held it out in front of himself and let it unfold, Daniel saw that it was an African outfit. It was bright white, with bold embroidery like he had seen on many other African outfits. Someone had taken great care in sewing this outfit, however. The white cloth had all sorts of intricate patterns on it when Daniel looked at it closely.

"Here," he said handing it to Daniel. "Wear this tomorrow when you come into the park.

"Thank you," Daniel said in awe.

Daniel opened his duffel bag, wrapped up his drum, and carefully placed it inside. Then he folded up the African outfit and placed it in on top. He gave Bro. Babatunde the bag of vegetables and Bro. Babatunde thanked him. As he set off on the path, Bro. Babatunde called after him.

"Bro. Daniel."

Daniel turned around. The duffel bag weighed heavy on his shoulder, but not as heavy as the burden he had been carrying.

"Peace be unto you."

"Peace to you, too Bro. Babatunde," as he walked out of the park. He knew that Bro. Babatunde would be praying for him, too.

IX

When Daniel got home, he went to the kitchen and heated up the dinner Grandma had left for him. Should he call Jerome? Should he go over to his house? Maybe he should just forget the whole thing. Why should he have to try to make amends with Jerome? He hadn't started anything. As a matter of fact, he had tried to help keep Jerome out of trouble. Though he wasn't really hungry, Daniel ate as much as he could, then washed his dishes and put the food up. Then he made up his mind that he would give Jerome a call.

As he was washing his hands, the door bell rang.

"I'll get that, Daniel, said Grandma

From the kitchen, Daniel could hear the door creak as Grandma opened it.

"Well hello, Jerome. How are you doing?"

"Good evening, Mrs. Williams," said Jerome in his most respectful voice. "Is Daniel available."

"Yes, he is. Come on in. Daniel..." she called.

Daniel walked from the kitchen through the front hall to the door.

"Daniel, I'm going upstairs. Y'all don't stay down here too late. Your mother will be home in an hour."

"Okay, Grandma."

As she walked up the stairs, Daniel turned back around to look at Jerome. Jerome looked down at first, as if too embarrassed to look at Daniel in the eye. Then he looked at him, though apparently with much difficulty.

"Yo man…" said Jerome. "I'm not gonna stay long. I…I just wanted to say I'm sorry for acting the way I did at the community center. I shouldn't have gone off on you like that."

"It's cool, man," said Daniel. I'm glad you came by, cuz I was just about to pay you a visit."

"I went back and apologized to Mr. Smith, too. I know I was acting stupid and he had every reason to put me out."

"I'm glad you didn't get into too much trouble."

"Well, they called my mother and told her what happened. She put me on punishment, but I asked if I could just come over here to apologize."

"Maybe after you're off punishment, we can play some ball again," said Daniel.

"Cool," said Jerome. "Oh yeah, man… thanks."

"Thanks for what?" asked Daniel.

"Thanks for trying to keep me outta trouble, man. I knew you weren't gonna fight me. And I know it wasn't cuz you were scared of me or anything. I don't know what got into me. But thanks for looking out for me. Johnny told me you kicked the knife out of the way so the cop wouldn't see it. I coulda been arrested and been charged with a felony for having a weapon. Thanks man…you've always had my back."

"No problem, man. I'm just glad the officer got there before it went any further."

The two boys laughed and shook hands.

"I know I'm always messin' with you…you know…about the rites of passage and the drumming. But the truth is, I really respect you for doing that stuff. I mean…I think I wanna go through the rites of passage."

Daniel smiled from ear to ear. "They're starting a new group in the fall. You can sign up at the community center!"

"Alright, man. I gotta get back home. I don't wanna test my mother. She was real upset after talking with that cop."

"See you later," said Daniel, opening the door. Jerome left and disappeared into the night.

X

The next day, Daniel woke just before sunrise. He washed his face, eyes, ears, and nose. Then he prayed and meditated using the drummer's breathing technique. He was very careful to follow all of Bro. Babatunde's instructions. He helped his Grandmother in the garden and cleaned up the kitchen and the living room. Going without food all day was starting to really take its toll, for he had never done this before. During the last three days of the rites of passage, the boys had to fast for three days, but only sunup to sundown. Now he had to go the whole day. Focusing on work around the house had kept his mind off of food for awhile, but now the hunger pains were beginning to really be felt.

After being in the yard and garden with Grandma for most of the morning, he chose to clean up his room for the latter part of the afternoon. He then took a shower. When he stepped out of the bathroom, there on his bed was the outfit that Bro. Babatunde had given him to wear. He had carefully laid it there before he had gotten in the shower. He put on the wide-leg drummer pants, then he slipped the dashiki over his head, and a pair of sandals on his feet. The outfit felt so clean and light. It made Daniel feel different. The outfit had a ceremonial feel to it. But something was missing and he couldn't quite put his finger on it. Since it was already 7:00, he didn't have time to sit around and think about what was missing. He sat on the edge of his bed, carefully wrapped up the djembe drum and placed it in his duffel bag.

He walked downstairs to the kitchen where Grandma was in front of the stove preparing dinner.

"Daniel!" she said in surprise looking him from head to toe. "What a wonderful outfit. Where did you get it?"

"Bro. Babatunde gave it to me. I have a special lesson today and he told me to wear it."

"Do you want to have some dinner before you go? It's just about ready."

Daniel's stomach growled. It seemed like his sense of smell was even more acute as he took in wonderful aroma of macaroni and cheese, greens, and baked chicken.

"No," he said reluctantly. "I'm not supposed to eat anything today. That's what Bro. Babatunde told me."

"Did he say why?"

"No. Just that its part of the lesson.

Kinda like when we had to fast during the rites of passage."

"Okay," said Grandma reaching into the refrigerator. "Well take this bottle of water and make sure you drink plenty of it."

Daniel took the bottle of water and placed in the side pouch of his duffel bag. He kissed Grandma on the cheek and headed toward the front door. As he opened the door he still felt like something was missing. But it was already after seven and he didn't have time to spare. As he walked down the front walk to the driveway, he heard the front door open.

"Daniel?!" called Grandma. "Wait," she said walking out to him. She was holding something in front of her. "Here, put this on." In her hands was the talisman that he had been given after completing his rites of passage. He bent his head down and she placed it over his head, then straightened it in the center of his chest.

"You look so handsome, son," she said smiling proudly. "Now go on...don't be late."

Daniel no longer felt as though he was missing something. As he walked down the sidewalk toward the park, he held the talisman in front of him studying it carefully. The brown leather on it smelled fresh. The carefully stitched symbol of the *gye gname* had new value to him as he remembered that it meant, "Supreme God."

Walking down Independence Avenue, he passed by all the familiar shops. He seemed to draw a lot of attention with his outfit. Mr. Jackson was standing outside the General Store sweeping.

"Hi, Mr. Jackson," he said

"How ya doing today, Daniel? That's a sharp outfit you got on there."

"Thanks," he said smiling proudly as he continued down the sidewalk.

Upon entering the gates of Heritage Park, he stopped and looked out over the pond and the trees. The sun sat just above the trees and was making its daily descent. Daniel closed his eyes, took a deep breath then let it out. As he began walking again, he heard a drum roll. It was Bro. Babatunde calling him. A very unique and distinct rhythm followed. Daniel hadn't heard it before, but it was clearly Bro. Babatunde's style. As he neared the oak tree, Bro. Babatunde started shouting, calling out as he beat the drum. But he wasn't speaking to Daniel and no one else was around. Whatever, he was saying, Daniel could tell it wasn't English. Bro. Babatunde was wearing a bright white outfit just like the one he had given Daniel.

Daniel walked up to the oak tree. Saying nothing, he picked up the folding chair that was leaning against the tree. He unfolded it and sat down to unpack his drum. Bro. Babatunde continued chanting and then brought his drumming to a close. He picked up a small hand towel and wiped his forehead. Then he looked at Daniel.

"You have followed my instructions today?" he asked.

"Yes," said Daniel pulling the sheet from around his drum.

"Very well, we are ready."

Daniel began his stretches. While he did Bro. Babatunde sat in his chair, eyes closed apparently meditating. When Daniel finished stretching Bro. Babatunde opened his eyes and stood up. He looked at Daniel, but said nothing.

"I am ready," said Daniel looking him right in the eyes. Then he took his drum, which was sitting beside him, and positioned it between his knees.

Bro. Babatunde, still said nothing. He reached into his worn leather bag and pulled out a wooden cup and his water bottle. He poured some water into the wooden cup and set the bottle down. Arms stretched, he held the cup up and looked up to the heavens. Again he began to shout words that Daniel didn't not understand. Though He didn't understand the words, Daniel could tell that these were words of power.

Bro. Babatunde then walked in front of Daniel and poured a few drops of water into the ground. He then walked around behind Daniel and did the same. Then he walked on Daniel's left and right side and poured drops of water uttering more words of power. Then he took a deep breath and poured the remaining water into the ground as he exhaled.

He took his seat, picked up his drum and positioned it between his knees.

"Play as I play," said Bro. Babatunde. "Some rhythms will be familiar, and other won't. Just follow along."

Daniel nodded.

"As the Spirit begins to move, close your eyes and keep them closed. You will know when to open them again."

Bro. Babatunde closed his eyes, rubbed his hands together for a moment, then began to play. Every few beats, Bro. Babatunde played the deep bass tone. Daniel followed him closely and effortlessly. The bass tones began to resonate in his being. The high and low tones were blending together perfectly. As Daniel continued to play the rhythm behind Bro. Babatunde, the Master Drummer began to add accompanying rhythms to the basic rhythm. Everything was flowing and the two were communicating on a higher level.

Daniel slowly closed his eyes, taking it all in. His heart rate increased, but his breathing was still controlled. He felt the life force energy rising from his solar plexis. It moved up and down his spine into his head and out through his arms and hands. The feeling was indescribable. His body was pulsating within and he felt like pure energy. He began to see flickering lights, just as he had in his basement.

Then, his stomach felt as though it was dropping as if he were going down a giant hill on a roller coaster. It was the same presence that sought to take him away against his will before. This time, he surrendered. His body quivered, but within, he was unmoved. His courage prevailed. He was no longer sitting under the oak tree, though his body was still there beating the drum. He could no longer hear the drums, but he could still feel the vibrations. The flickering lights came together to form the sun once again. There beneath the sun, as before was a large group of people. It was like a celebration. The people were chanting, jumping up and down, and waving their hands. Try as he might, he could not see past them into the circle. But he could now hear the drumming that had them jumping and dancing. It was the same beat he and Bro. Babatunde had been playing. The sound was growing in its volume. Daniel put his hands on the shoulders of two of the people in front of him. It was a man and a woman. They both turned around and looked at him.

Their eyes got wide with even greater excitement when they saw Daniel. They moved aside and motioned for him to go through the crowd. As these two stepped aside others turned around and saw him. They too, looked with excitement upon him as if he was a guest of honor or some sort of royal dignitary. The sea of people in the cypher parted until Daniel came all the way through. After the last person was out of the way, Daniel saw people in masks and costumes in a smaller circle dancing energetically as if they were endowed with the same indwelling presence that had brought Daniel to this place. They were dancing and shouting. The words they were shouting and the cadence in which they shouted sounded very similar to what Bro. Babatunde had been chanting. The dancers continued their dancing and shouting.

Then one of the dancers came to Daniel with arms outstretched. He took Daniel by both of his hands and walked him toward the circle. In rhythmic order, the dancers began to part the smaller circle and Daniel walked through. Inside of this cypher was a circle of six drummers. The drummers were wearing the same white outfit that Daniel was. They were walking and dancing with their drums which were strapped over their shoulders with a thick belt of cloth. They moved out and in to the rhythm of the beat, keeping the circle intact.

Daniel was amazed at what he saw. Never before had he even imagined such a scene. The rhythm was captivating, the energy was elevating, and the spirit was liberating.

All of a sudden, the drummers parted the circle. There in the middle was another drummer. He was dressed as the others but with a royal strip of blue and purple cloth draped over his shoulder His smooth dark skin was radiant in the sunlight and striking in contrast to the white outfit he wore. His eyes were glowing as he stared at Daniel. The man looked strangely familiar. Daniel did a double-take and it was all clear to him now. The man in the middle, the drummer with the royal cloth, was his father.

The floodgates opened and tears poured from his eyes which were still open, transfixed on the man he thought he would never see again.

"One day we'll see him again," Grandma had told him when he cried at the funeral. "Only his body is gone, not his Spirit."

The mixed emotions Daniel had felt ebbed away and he was filled with the love that he felt had always been missing since his father left. His father took the drum strap from around his neck and placed it on the ground. He walked toward Daniel with with arms outstretched. Daniel, still overwhelmed with emotion, was unable to move. His father came to him and embraced him.

Nine years of pain, confusion, and disillusionment no longer mattered or even existed. There was a healing quality in his father's embrace. The drummers stopped drumming and the dancers stopped dancing. The people slowly departed. Then Daniel's father looked him deeply in the eyes. "Daniel, it is so good to see you...and so good to have you see me. I knew you would have the courage to come."

Though the pain was gone, there were still unanswered questions in Daniel's mind.

"It was just like Grandma said. She said I would see you again."

"She is a very wise and faithful woman. I am so thankful that she is my mother."

"But why did you have to leave? Why did you have to go?"

"She shared the story with you?"

"Yes."

"Daniel, a man must live his life according to the laws of God and the path God has laid. I took an oath to serve and protect my family and my community. I didn't make that oath to the police department. I made that oath to God. I wanted to make the streets clean so that you would grow up in a safe and loving environment."

"It just doesn't seem fair," said Daniel.

"There are some things that are worth dying for, Daniel. When those brothers...those lost brothers, took that little boy hostage, I had to respond. That little boy reminded me of *you*. It is because I was willing to step forward, that his life was spared. And right now, that same boy has trouble understanding why God spared his life. But you're in a position to help him. His name is Jerome."

Daniel had no idea. The two had met in fifth grade. Jerome had never told him about his past.

"It was not just by chance that you two are friends. You were led to one another, to be there for one another."

"But he never told me," said Daniel.

"Because it was such a traumatic experience, there is much that he doesn't remember, just as there was much about my death that you didn't remember. His mother chose not to tell him the details because it was difficult for her, too."

"How am I supposed to live the rest of my life without a father?" asked Daniel.

"God has sent and will send you people to guide you on the right path. You must embrace the love and wisdom they share."

"What about Bro. Babatunde? Is he one of those people sent to give me guidance?"

"Yes, but he has a story all his own. He helped me to contact you."

"Why can't you stay with us?" Daniel pleaded.

"It just cannot be that way. I pleaded just as you have. I am just thankful that I was able to contact you here."

"Will I be able to see you again?"

"I don't know if we can ever come here again. But when you look in the midnight sky and see a star twinkling, think of me. When you are walking in the park and the air is calm and all of sudden there is a breeze, think of me. When Bro. Babatunde instructs you in the drum, or you are practicing in the basement, think of me. For it is your thoughts of me which keep me alive. The Ancestors have said that if you say the names of the departed they never die."

For a moment Daniel felt dismayed.

"All the those times you felt alone...you must understand, you were never alone. And there will be more difficult times. But always remember, you are never alone."

His father's words comforted him. All the other unanswered questions no longer mattered now. The dancers and the drummers circled around them once again. The rhythms and chanting filled the air once again.

"I am going the way of all of our Ancestors. Be strong, Daniel, and show yourself to be a man. Walk in the path of the Most High in everything you do and you will be blessed. Soon, we will meet again," said his father as the drummers enclosed themselves around him again.

Daniel wanted to come with him, but knew that it was not yet time. Then the dancers encircled themselves around the drummers and the people encircled themselves around the dancers. Daniel looked up at the sun. It was shining bright upon his face. Then the light of the sun began to flicker. He felt the pulsing of the life-force energy throughout his body as it slightly quivered. He felt the touch of his hands beating the drum feverishly. His hands began to slow down until finally they stopped.

Daniel slowly opened his eyes. He looked at his hands. They were trembling.

"Bro. Daniel. You have returned." said Bro. Babatunde wiping Daniel's tear-stained face with a hand towel. Daniel was still just coming back to himself. Then he looked at Bro. Babatunde deeply in the eyes?

"Who are you?" Daniel asked, sensing that he was more than what he appeared. His voice quivered with emotion. He was so choked up, he could not muster his normal voice. "And how did you make all this happen?"

"Your eyes have been opened," said Bro. Babatunde. With a penetrating gaze, he looked into Daniel's soul. "You will recognize your brothers by the way they act and move throughout the world." There will be a strange force about them and unspoken answers in them."

Still confused, Daniel stared at Bro. Babatunde trying to look within him. Around Bro. Babatunde's head, Daniel could see a light. It was radiating his aura and Daniel could see his spirit.

"My name is Babatunde. My name means, *Father/Elder returns*. I was sent to you to help you reconnect to your roots. I was sent to you to help you make contact with your father."

"But...how did you know? How could you have known...that I wanted to see my father...even before you knew me?" asked Daniel.

"I was your father's teacher. I never told you because you were not ready. He told me about those that were seeking his life. He struggled to find the courage to take a stand.

He had me promise that if anything happened to him, that I would teach you. He told me to find you when you came of age."

Daniel could now see the age on Bro. Babatunde's face. He could see that it wasn't easy for Bro. Babatunde to revisit these memories.

"I, too, was deeply grieved by your father's death...so much so that I stopped teaching people the way of the drum." Bro. Babatunde let out a deep sigh. Then his face began to return to its normal energetic glow.

"But I am in constant contact with God and the Ancestors. It was revealed to me that you had come of age...and I was sent to find you. I have not taught anyone the way of the drum since your father."

It was all coming together for Daniel now, but he still had a few more questions.

"How is it that you can communicate like this...with God and the Ancestors?"

"There are others like me...I'm not the only one. Most people walk by us everyday, thinking us to be poor or homeless or just everyday people. There are so many more who must be awakened."

"But why was I chosen for this?"

"Partly because it was the desire of your heart and partly because of your ancestry. You see, you come from a long line of priests and drummers, young Daniel. You come from the Ashanti nation of Ghana.

Daniel was dumbfounded. He didn't know what to say.

"You have a good spirit, Daniel. You will do many great and wonderful things for your people and for Humanity," said Bro. Babatunde. "All of this is preparation."

Daniel sat for a moment, amazed at all that had just happened. A part of him tried to feel sad wondering when he would be able to see his father again. But his Higher Self emerged to reveal that he had just experienced a blessed encounter.

"I know you have many questions, but right now, you must go home and rest," said Bro. Babatunde.

Daniel couldn't argue with him. For though he still had many questions to ask, he felt terribly fatigued. As he packed up his things, he knew now, like never before, that his life had a purpose. A warm feeling of love and under-standing ran through his body.

When he finished packing, he looked at Bro. Babatunde. He didn't speak because they were communicating on a higher level. He just nodded to Bro. Babatunde offering him peace with his eyes rather than words from his mouth. Bro. Babatunde nodded in return. Daniel placed the duffel bag on his shoulder and began walking toward Independence Avenue.

The air was calm in Heritage Park as the sun set over the trees behind the pond. The grass looked a little greener and the trees more lush and full. Daniel felt the wind blow slightly. He smiled, for he knew that his past and his future somehow came together in that breeze.

GLOSSARY

Ankh (onk): an ancient Kemetic (Egyptian) symbol of everlasting life.

Beni Hasan (ben-ee hah-sahn): a city of ancient Kemet where the origins of the martial arts can be found written on the walls of the temple.

Djembe Drum (jim-bay): a drum made of wood and goat skin from West Africa.

Ghana (gon-nah): a small country on the west coast of Africa.

Gye gyame (jee-nee yah-may): ancient adinkra symbol used among the people of Ghana, West Africa; it refers to the Supreme God of the universe.

Hatshepsut (hat-shep-soot): a woman of ancient Kemet who emerged as the first woman Pharoah; her reign lasted for 21 years and was characterized by complete peace in the land.

Hotep (ho-tep): a Kemetic word meaning, "peace."

Ipet Isut (I-pet I-soot): an ancient learning center in Kemet located in the city of Waset; some 80,000 students came from all over Kemet and around the world to study the Sacred Sciences there.

Kemet (Ke-met): the original name for what is now called Egypt; it means, "land of the black/burnt-skinned people."

Ma'at (mo-ot): represented by a feather, Ma'at was the principle of truth.

Medu Neter (me-doo net-ter): the holy writings of the ancient Kemetans; the Greeks referred to them as hieroglyphics.

Obelisk (o-bel-isk): a tall, four-sided pole with a pyramid capstone; often built just outside of Kemetic temples; the Washington Monument is a replica of the Kemetic obelisk.

Ptahotep (tah-ho-tep): an ancient scribe in the king's court from Kemet; his writings represent the oldest complete text in the world (see *The Teachings of Ptahotep*).

Sacred Sciences: the secret studies of ancient Kemet including science, mathematics, astrology, alchemy, architecture, spirituality; referred to by the Greeks as the Mystery System.

Sankofa (san-ko-fah): ancient adinkra symbol used among the people of Ghana, West Africa; it refers to understanding one's history in order to go forth intelligently into the future.

Scales of Ma'at: on one side of the scales was placed a feather to represent truth and justice; on the other side of the scales was placed one's heart on the day of judgment; the idea was that one's pure heart should balance the scales and not tilt the scales.

Seven Principles of Ma'at: truth, justice, righteousness, reciprocity, balance order, harmony; the seven principles upon which a person's life was said to be judged.

Talisman (ta-lis-min): an object which serves as a reminder of an important event in one's life. Usually a necklace.

Tehuti (te-hoo-tee): known as a messenger in ancient Kemet; responsible for bringing the proper interpretation of the medu neter (holy writings).

The Teachings of Ptahotep A book co-authored by Asa Hilliard, Nia Damali and Larry Williams.

Waset (wah-sett): city of ancient Kemet [Egypt] where one of the greatest learning centers of the ancient world can be found.

About the Author

Chike Akua (Justin Fenwick) is a 1992 cum laude graduate of Hampton University. Bro. Akua has distinguished himself as an educator, lecturer, and author. In 1995, he was selected as

a **Teacher of the Year** for Newport News (Virginia) Public Schools. In 1996, the Dekalb County Board of Education (Atlanta, Georgia) awarded him the Achievement Award for teaching excellence and service to youth. Akua has since conducted system-wide staff development and was described as *"a master teacher."*

Selected as one of *Ebony* magazine's **"50 Leaders of Tomorrow"** (November, 1995), Akua has lectured at several of the nation's colleges and universities and has appeared on radio and television talk shows sharing his perspectives on education, spirituality, and uplift. Akua, a Christian minister and consultant with Imani Enterprises is the author of five books:

- *A Treasure Within: Stories of Remembrance & Rediscovery* (2001)
- *A Treasure Within: Parent/Teacher Resource Guide* (2001)
- *A Kwanzaa Awakening: Lessons for the Children* (2000)
- *A Million Under One: One Man's Perspective on the Million Man March* (1996)
- *The Autobiography of the African American Self* (1995)

Akua is a member of Victory Baptist Church (Stone Mountain, Georgia) where he teachers Sunday school and Afrocentric Christianity. He is currently pursuing graduate studies in education at Clark Atlanta University.

A
KWANZAA
AWAKENING

REVISED &
EXPANDED EDITION

LESSONS FOR THE CHILDREN

CHIKE AKUA
(JUSTIN FENWICK)

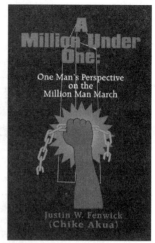

A Million Under One:

One Man's Perspective
on the
Million Man March

Justin W. Fenwick
(Chike Akua)

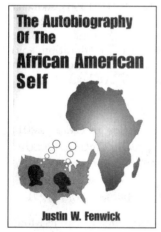

The Autobiography
Of The
African American
Self

Justin W. Fenwick

Parent/Teacher
Resource Guide

A TREASURE
WITHIN

STORIES OF REMEMBRANCE
& REDISCOVERY

CHIKE AKUA

Imani Enterprises/Chike Akua
3014 Hampton Club Way
Lithonia, Georgia 30038
770-323-1375
www.imanienterprises.org

MAIL ORDER
INVOICE

Mail To _____

Address _____

_____

Phone _____ **Fax** _____

Qty	Price	Item	Amount
	$15	The Treasure Within: Stories of Remembrance & Rediscovery	
	$15	The Treasure Within: Parent/Teacher Resource Guide	
	$15	A Kwanzaa Awakening: Lessons for the Children	
	$15	A Million Under One: One Man's Perspective on the Million Man March	
	$15	The Autobiography of the African American Self	
		SUBTOTAL	
		SHIPPING	
		TOTAL	

* Please make check or money order payable to: **Imani Enterprises**
* Please allow 2-4 weeks for delivery
* Add **SHIPPING CHARGES** of $4 for the first item and $1.50 for each additional item.